Bring to life the incredible characters of the world of "Zahara," where warriors in gleaming armor, mighty sorcerers, and elven and dwarven fighters clash with fierce dragons, dark orcs, and magical, mysterious creatures.

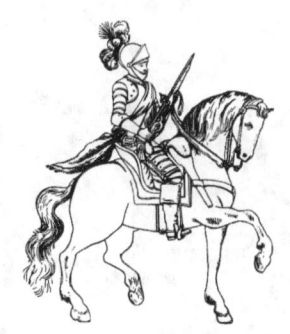

menteinteligente P.D
2024

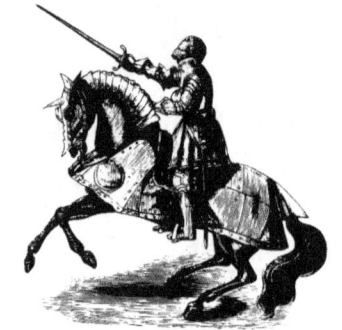

This Book Belongs to:

o- -|

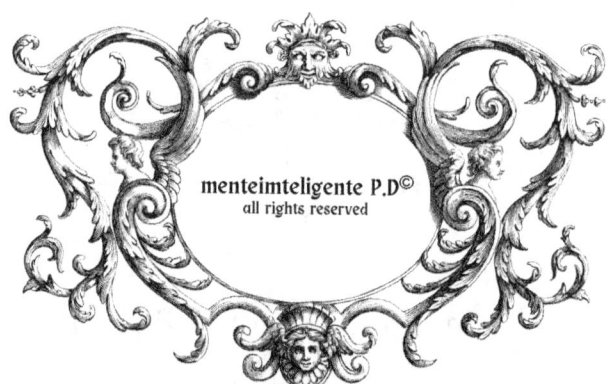

Test Color Page

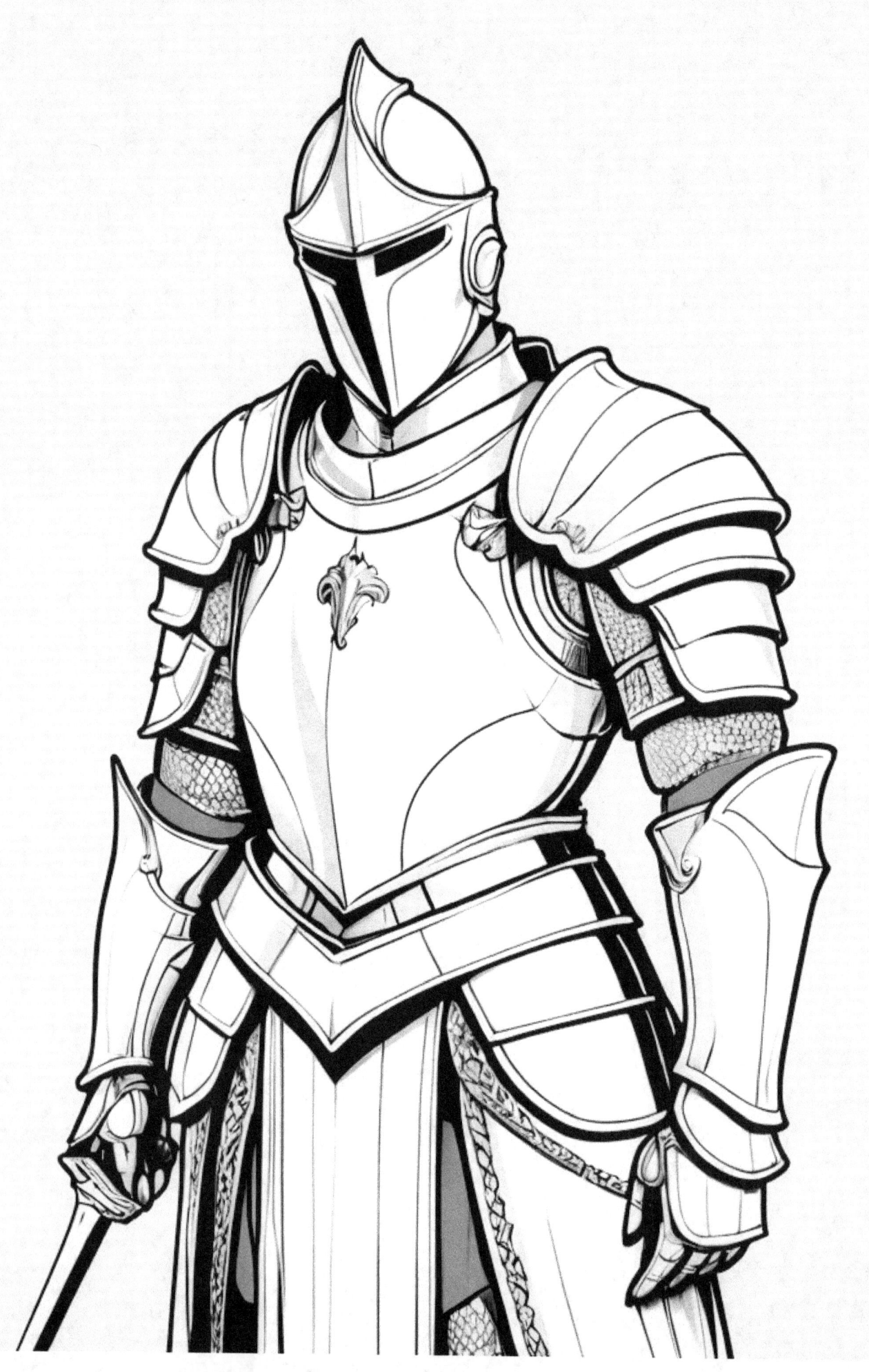

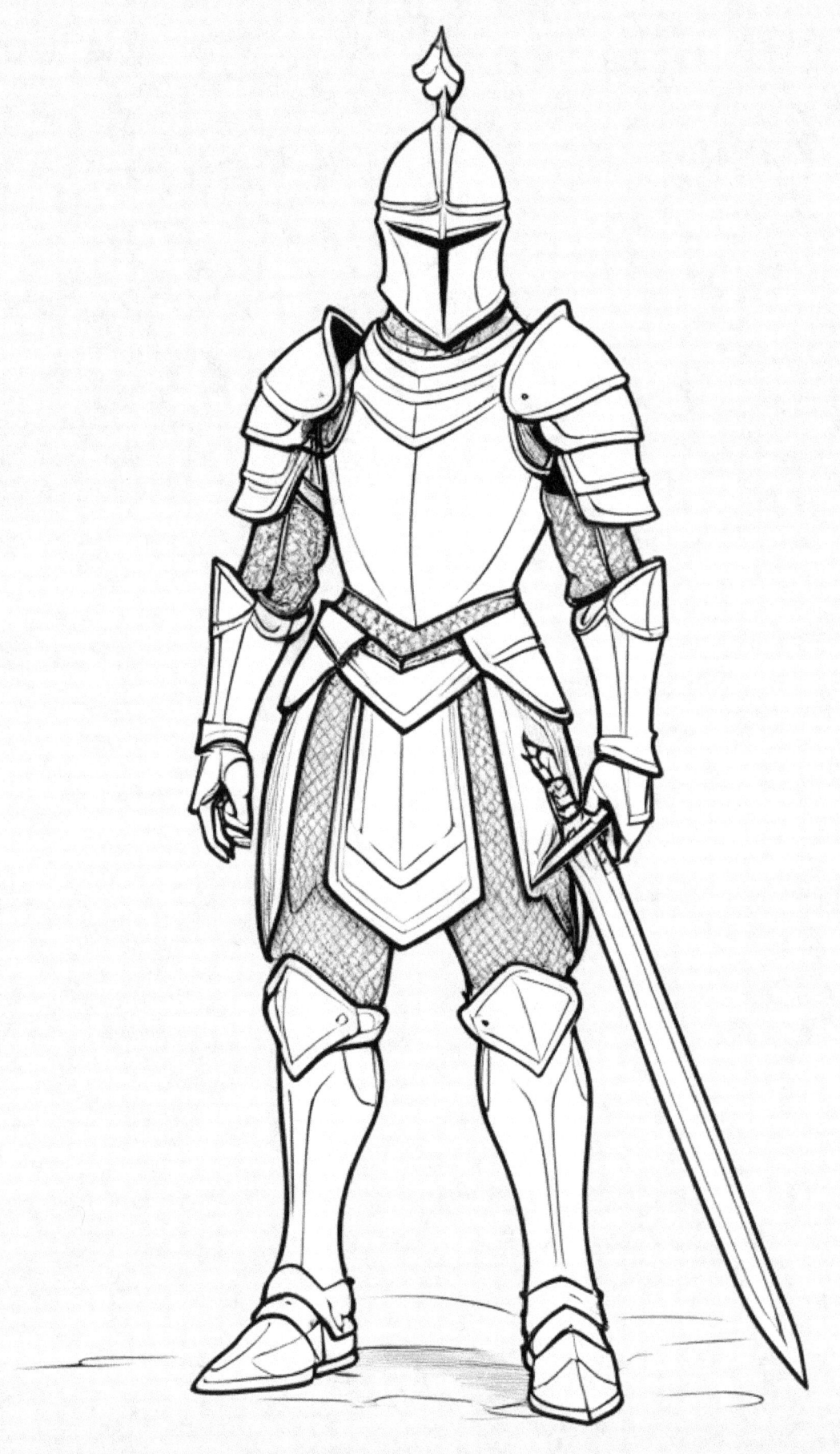

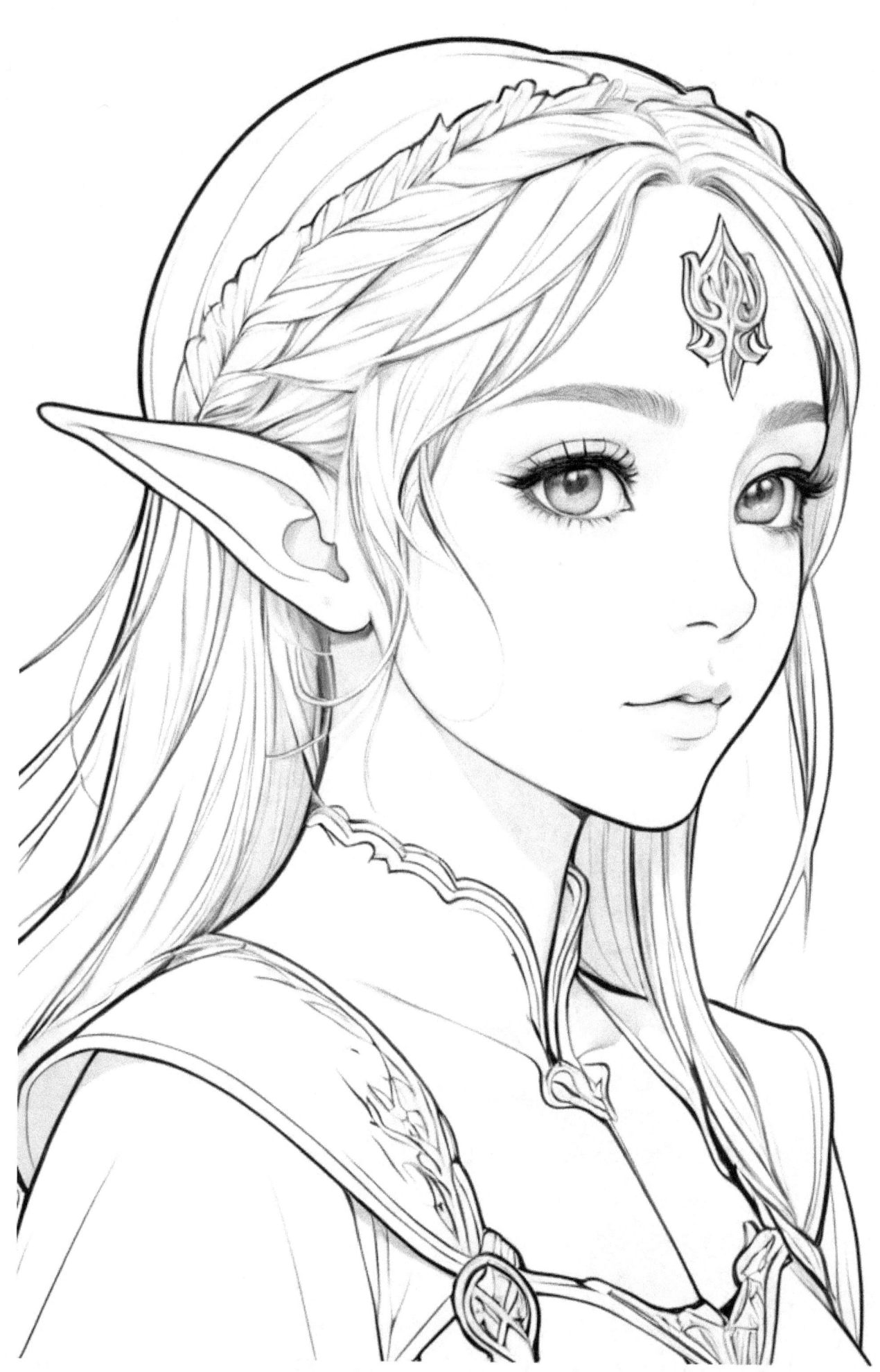

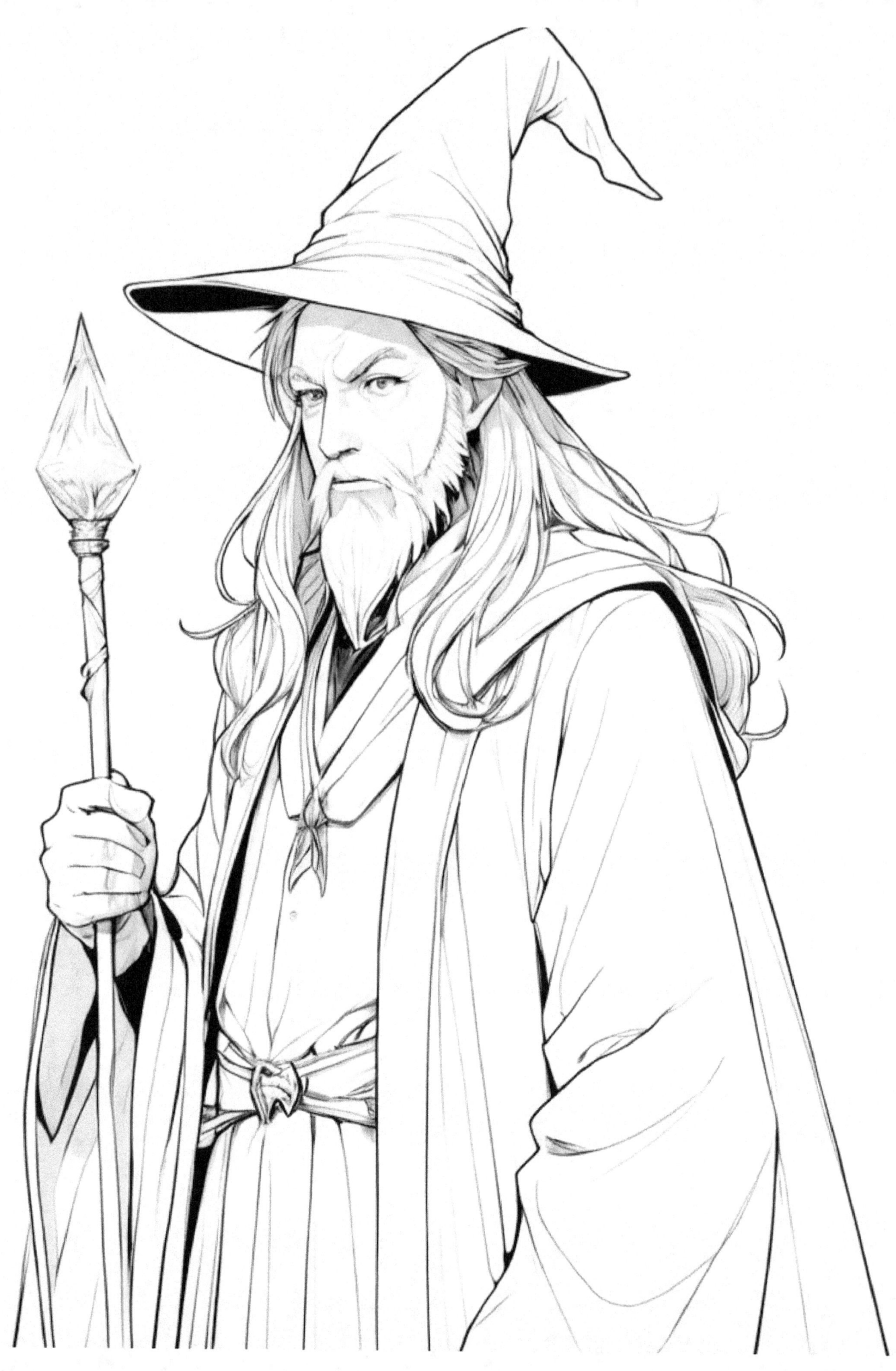

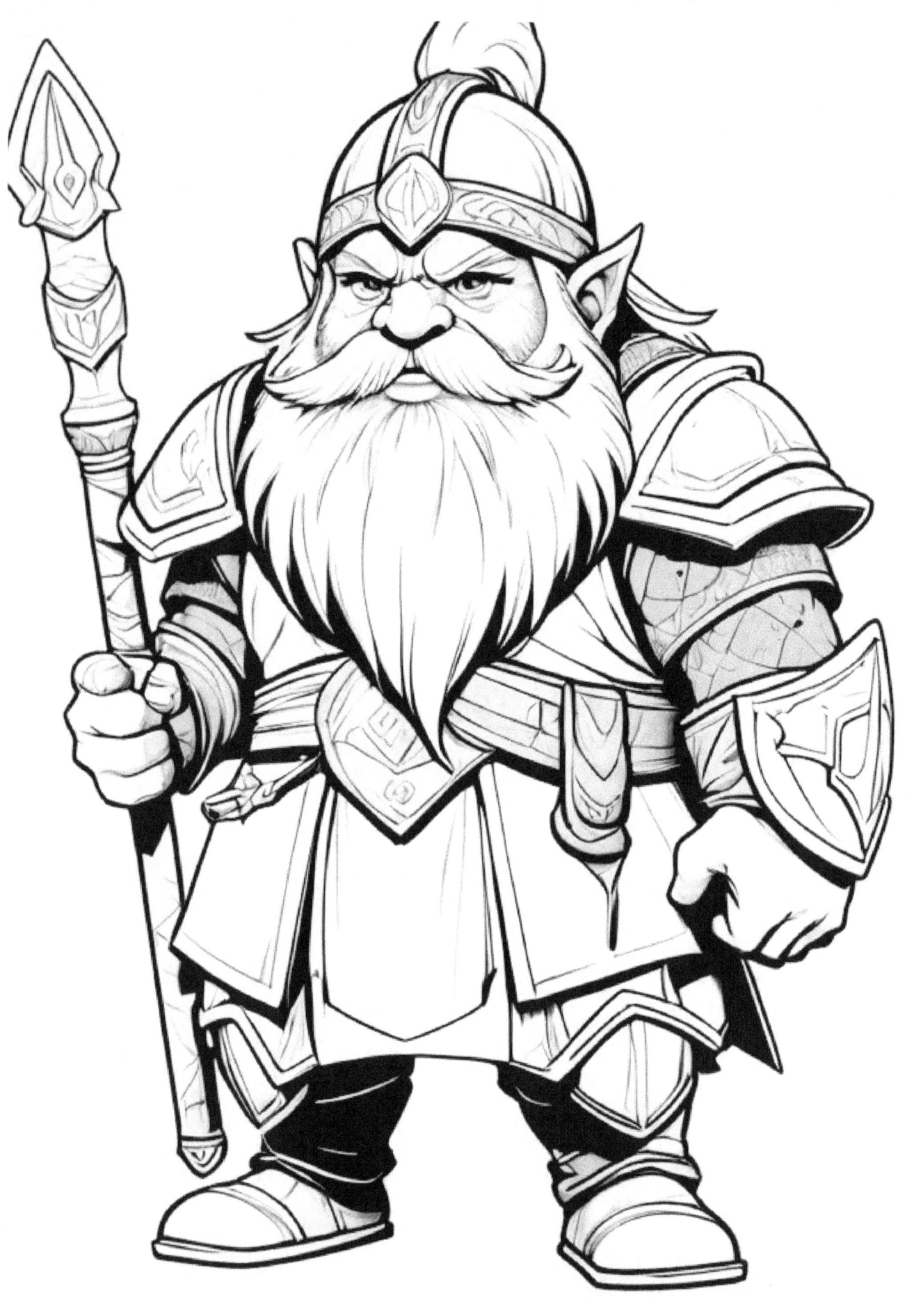

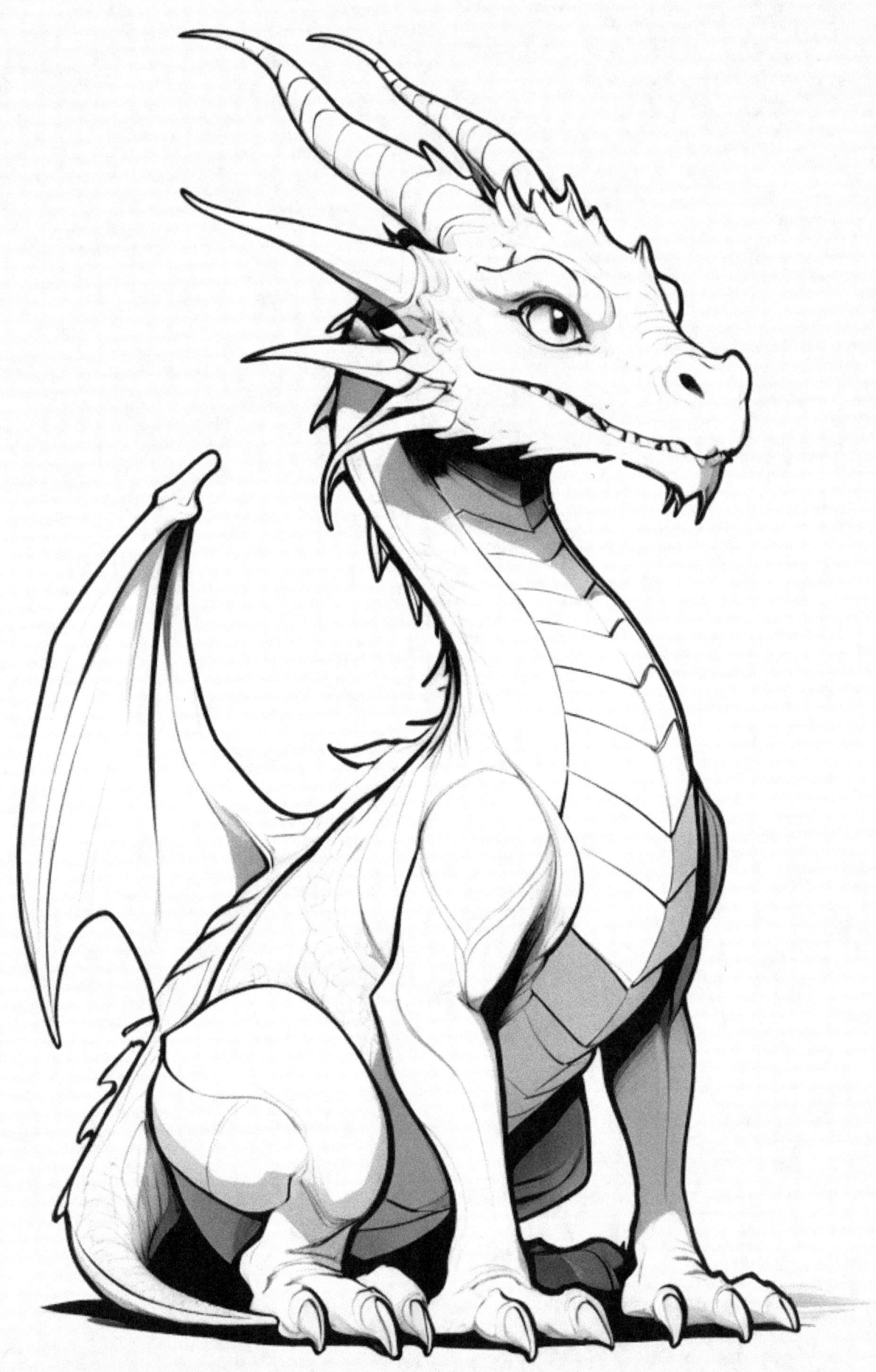

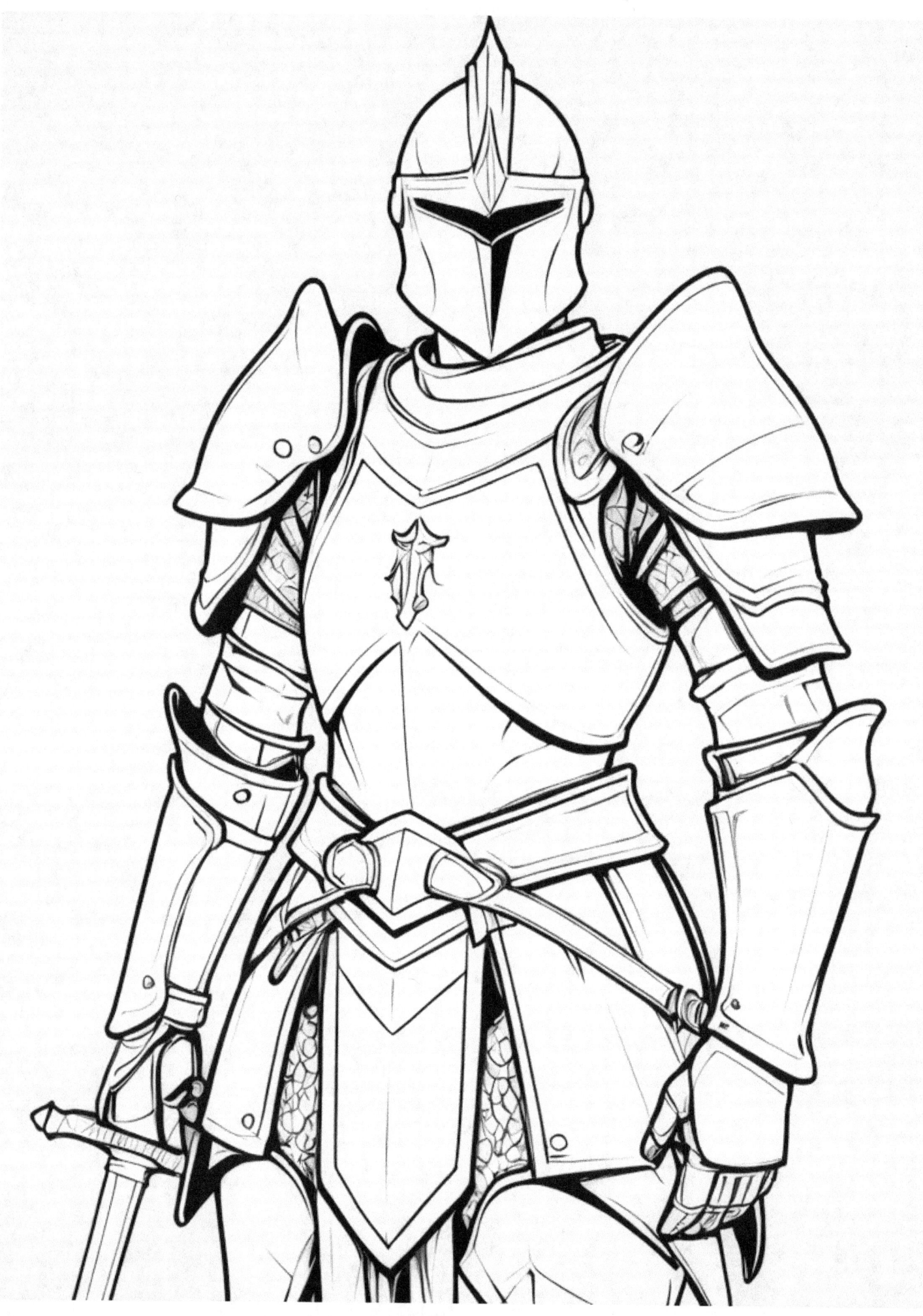

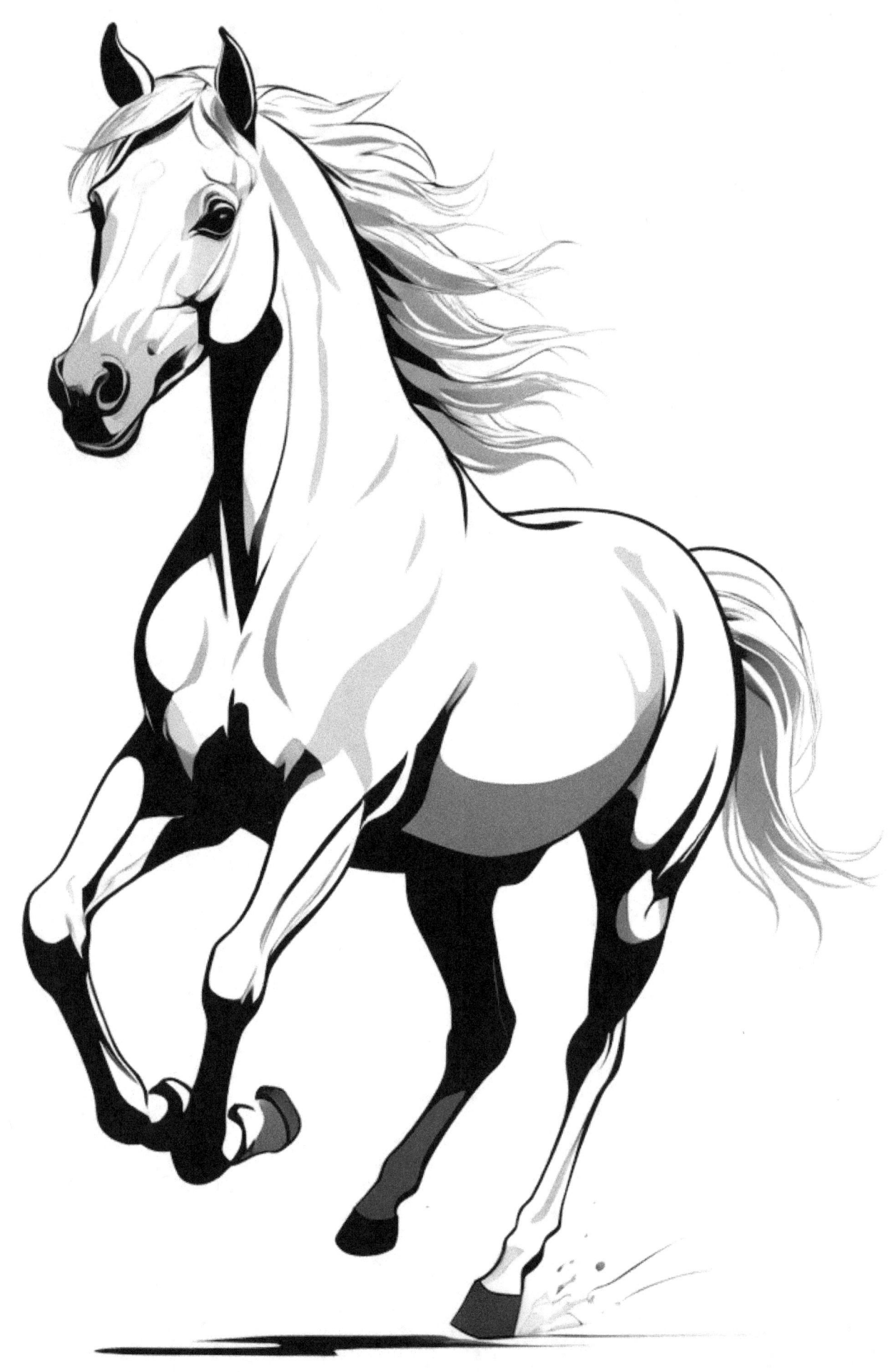

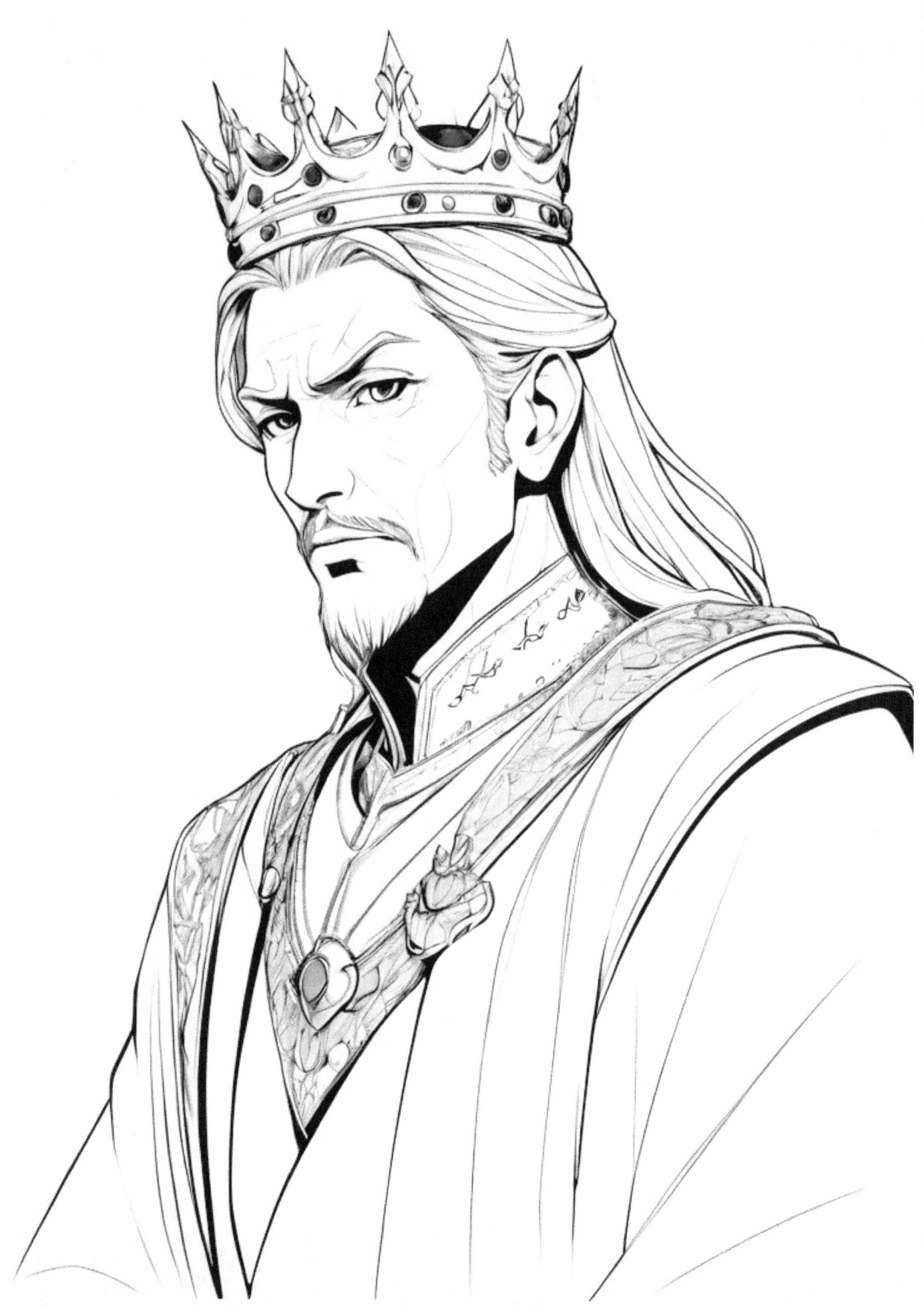

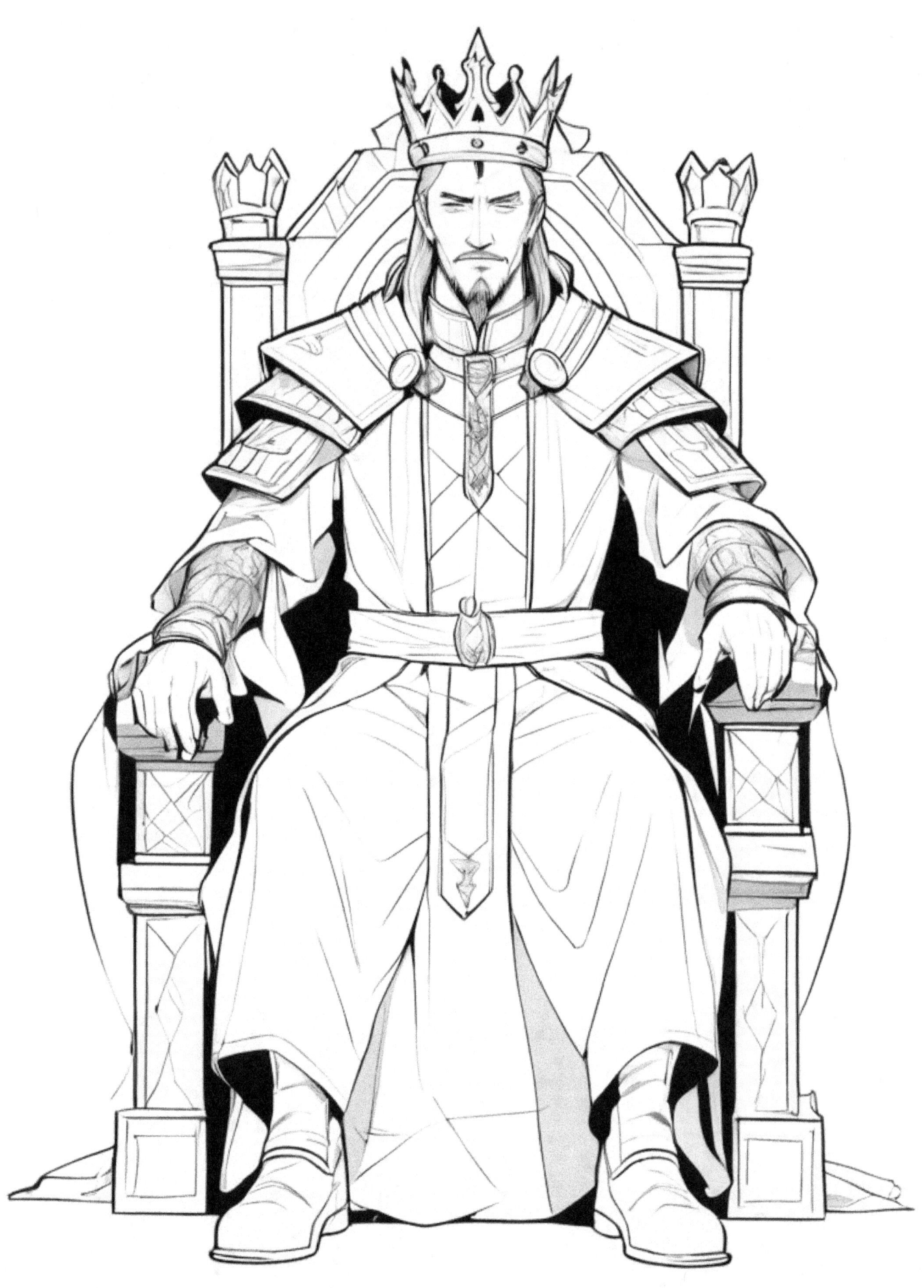

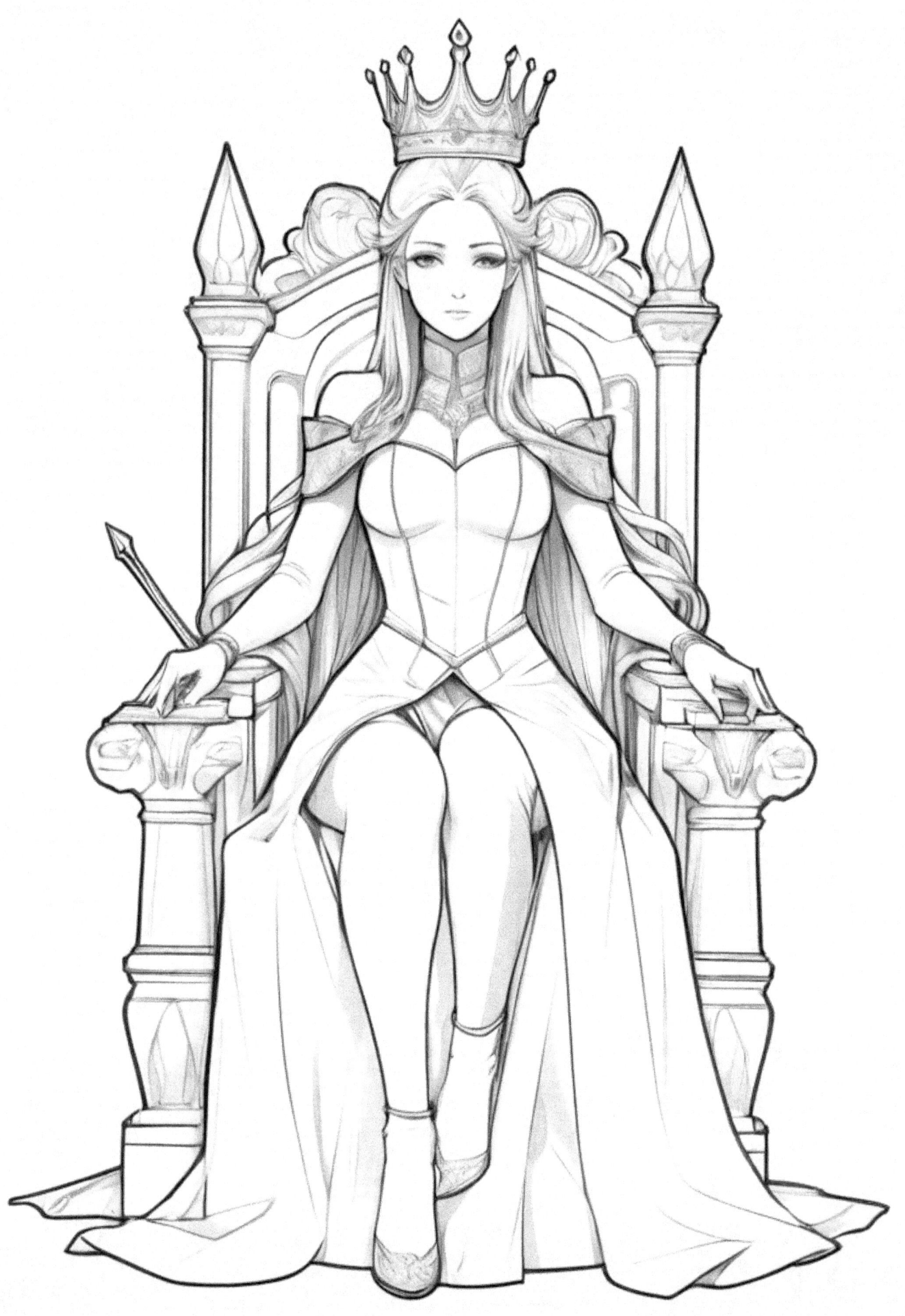

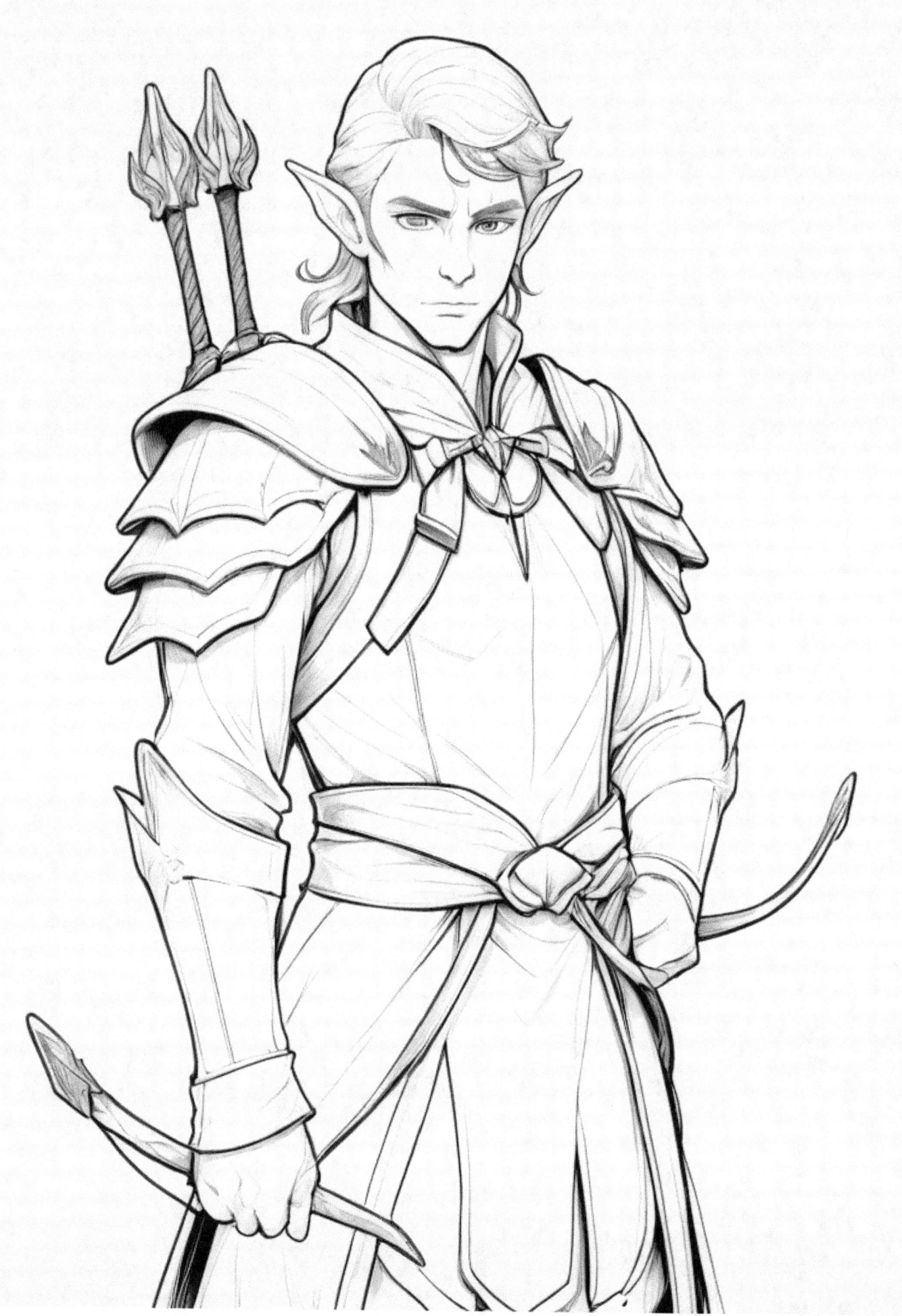

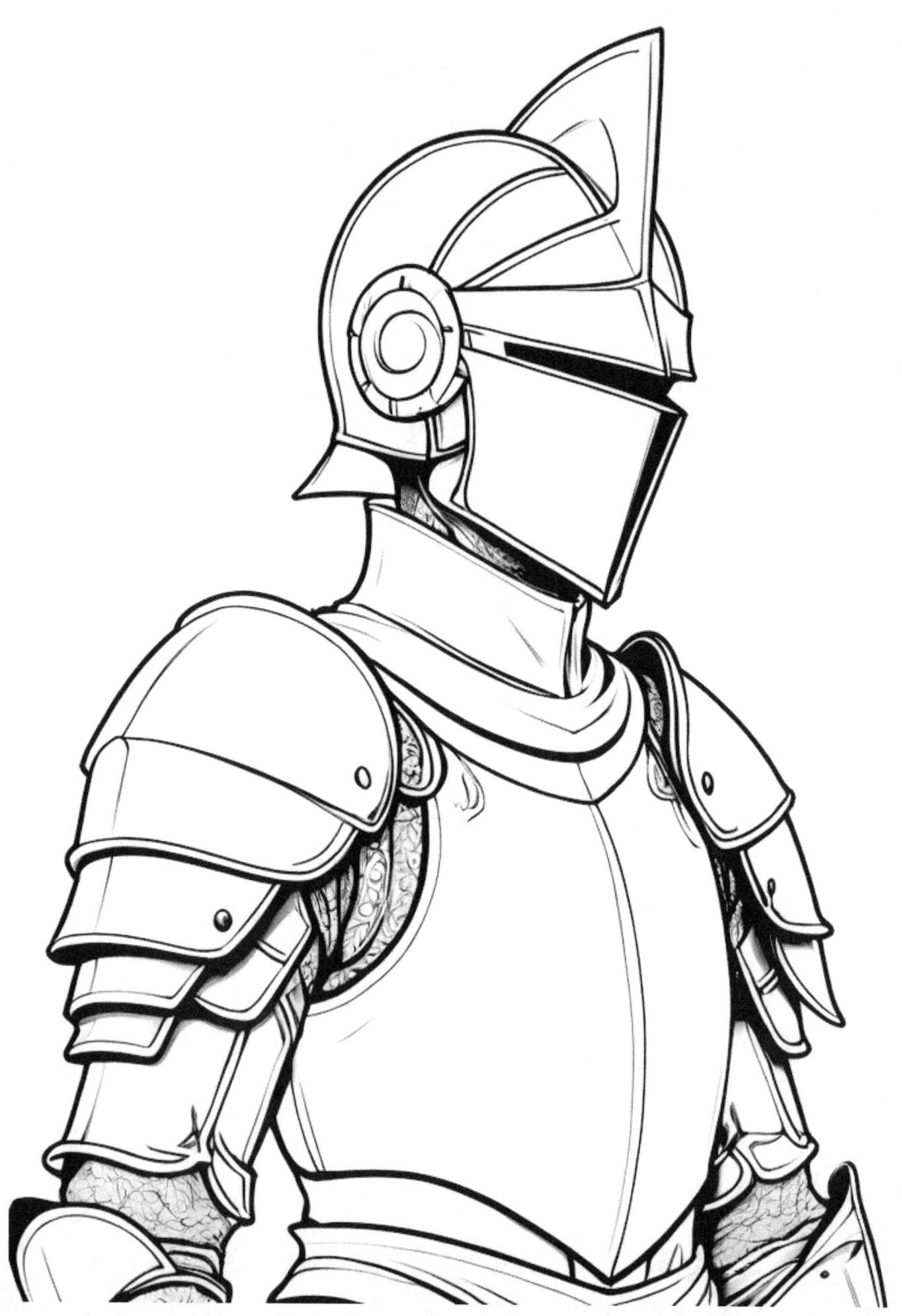

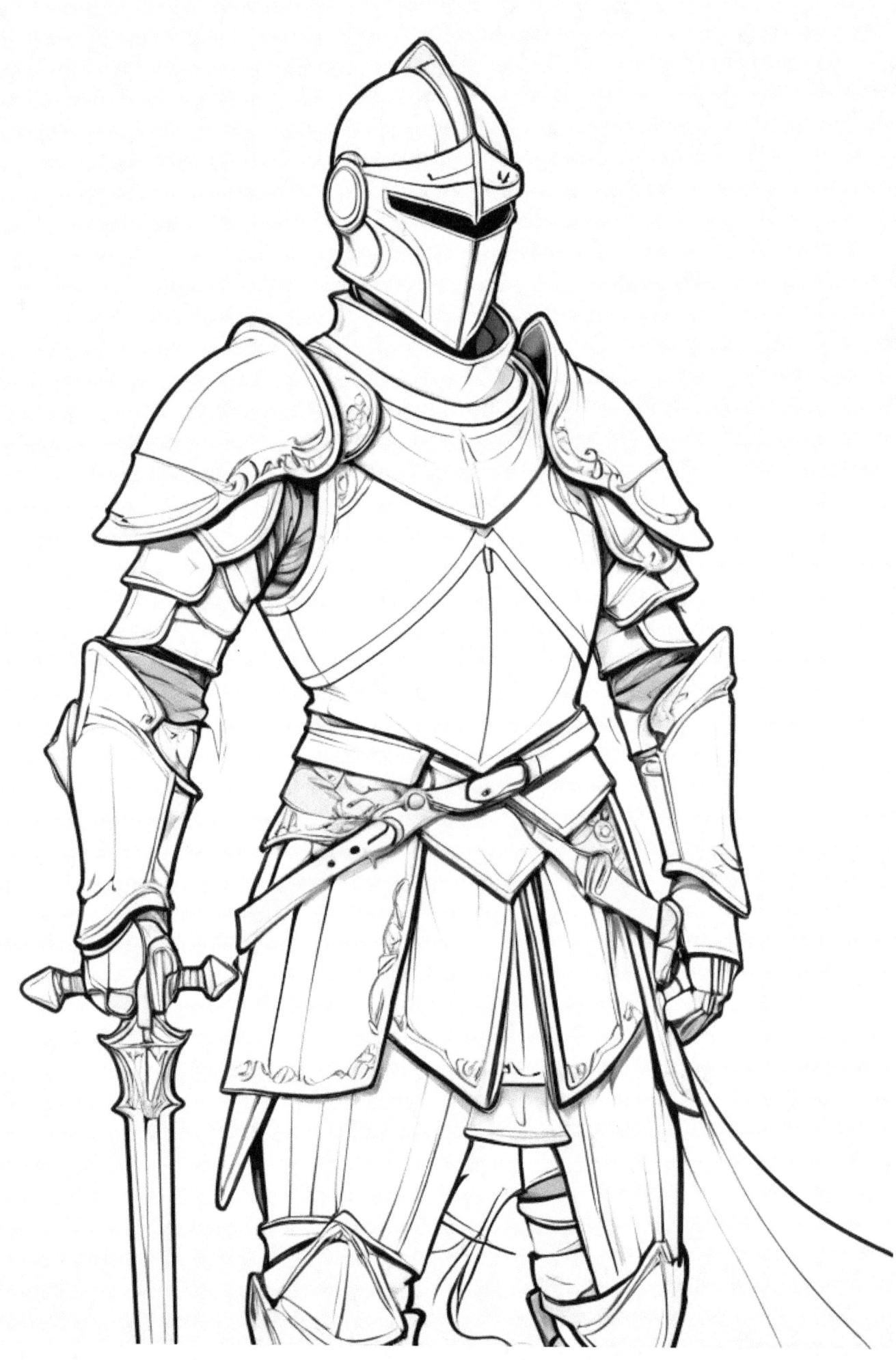

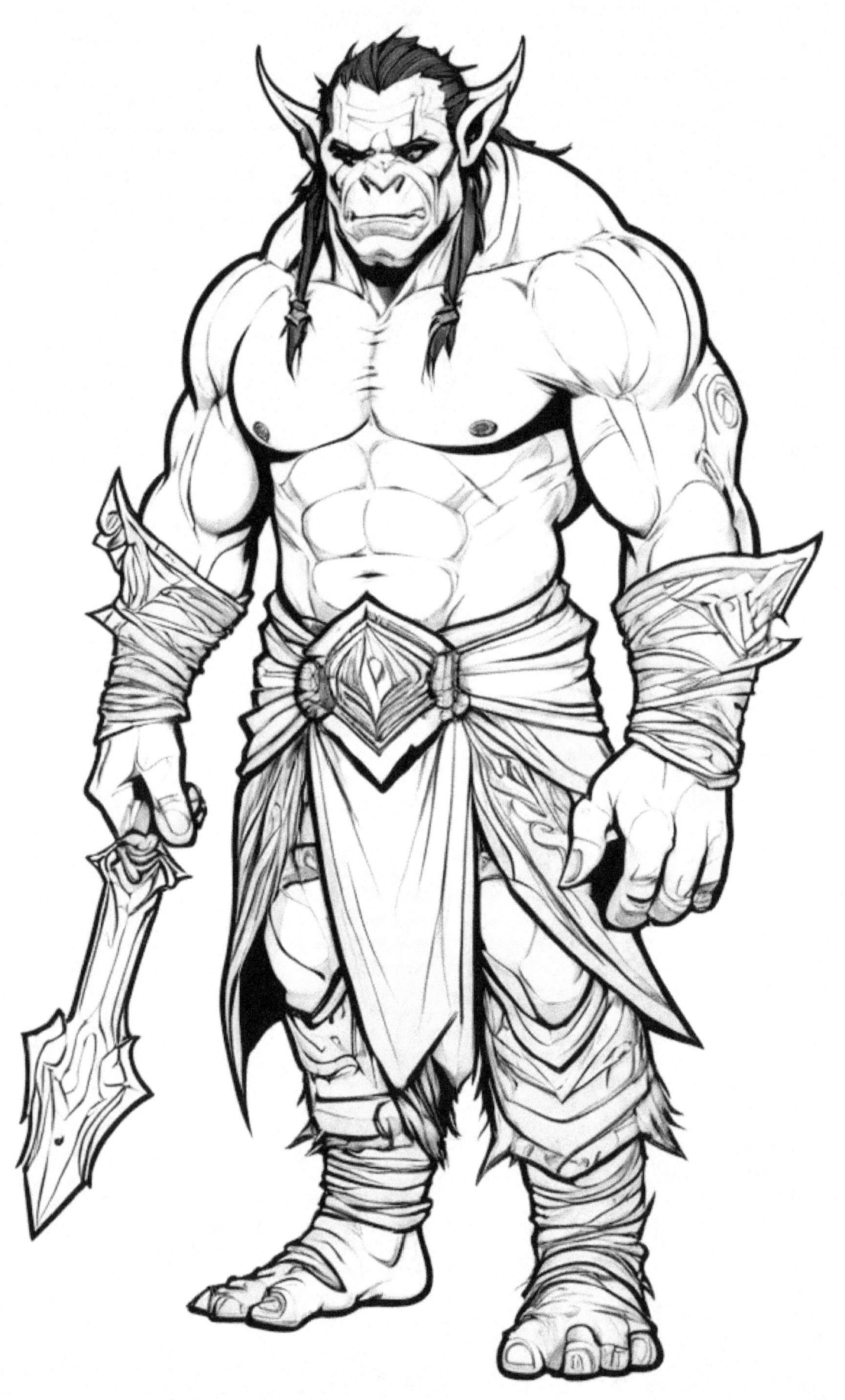

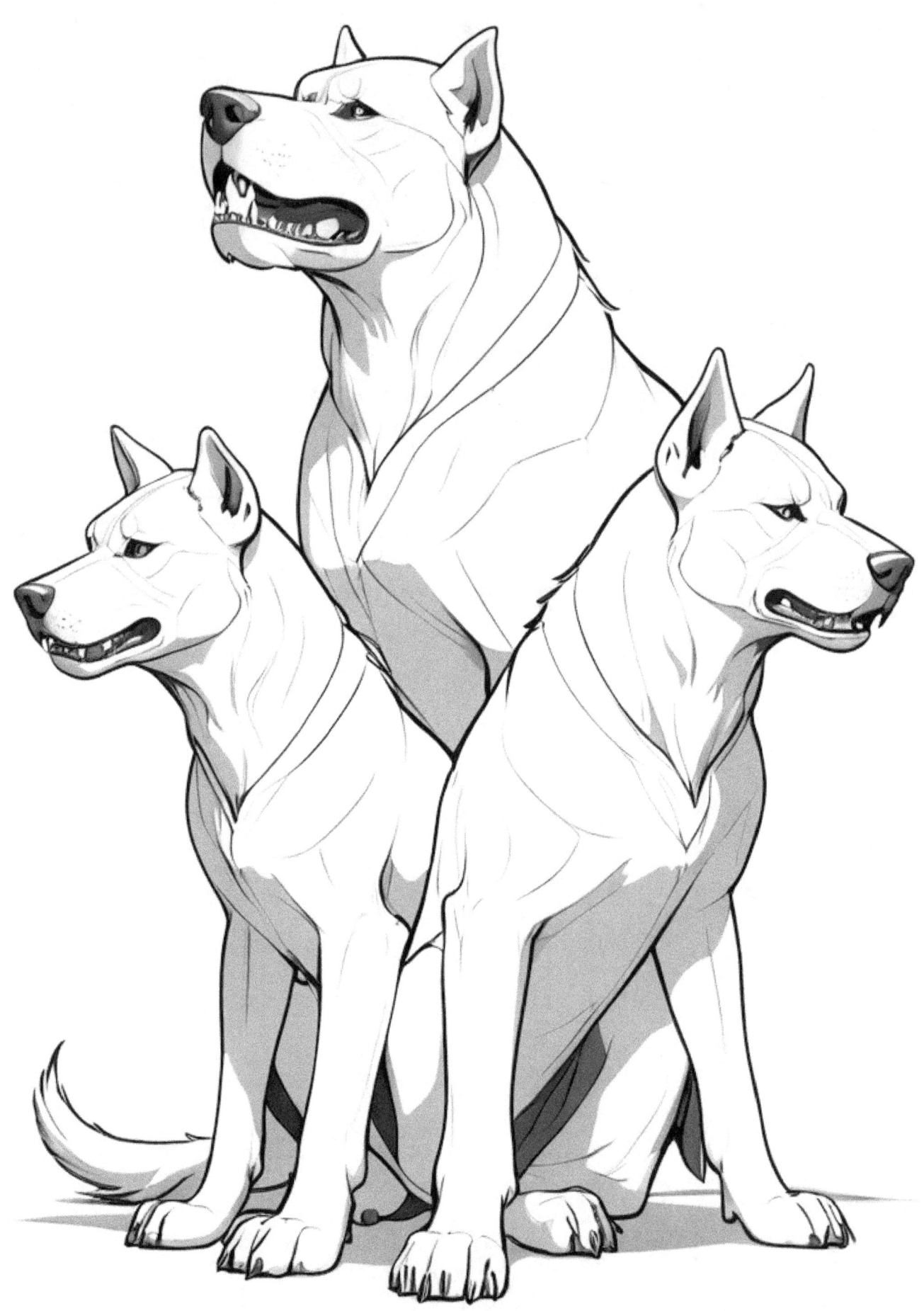

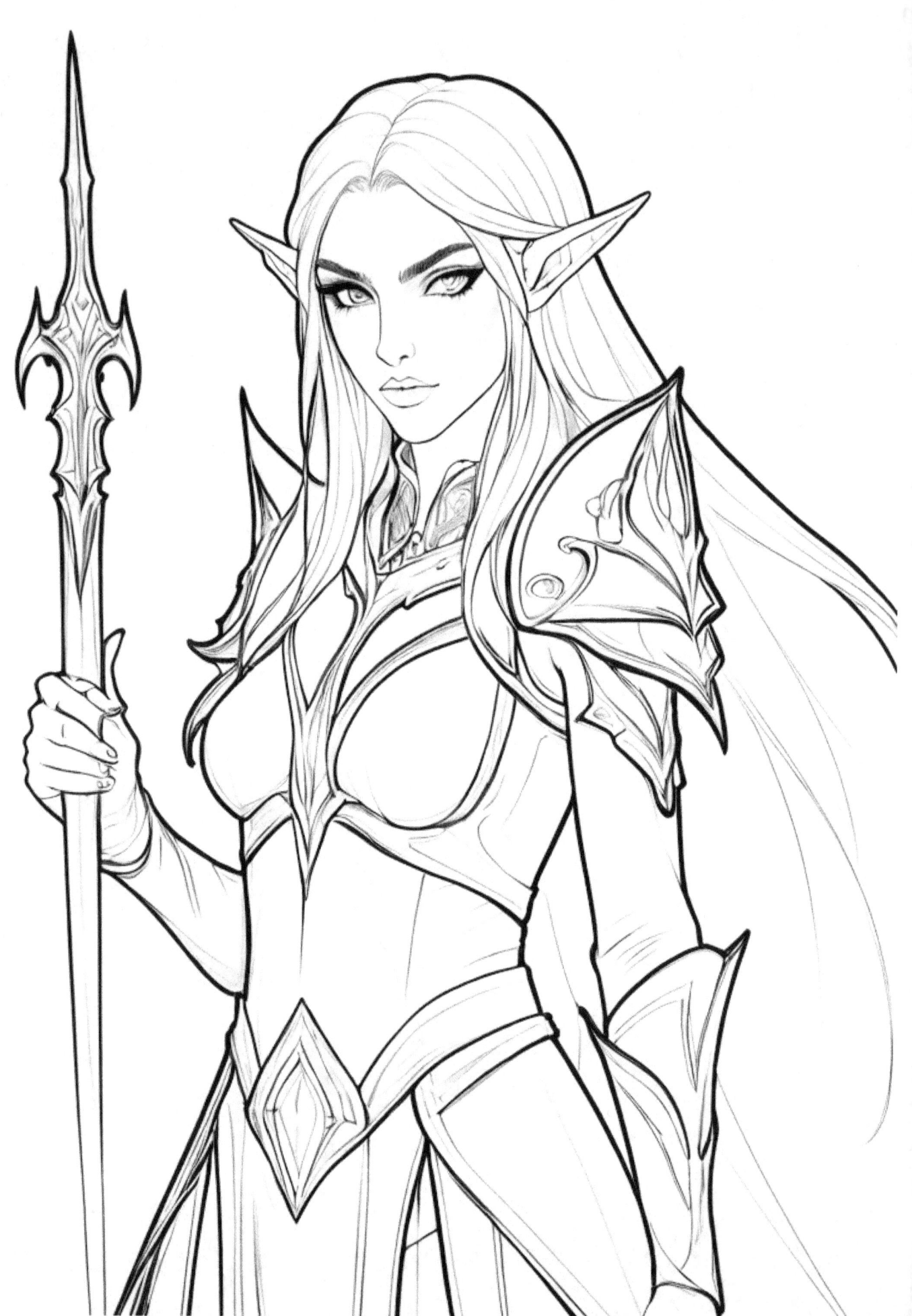

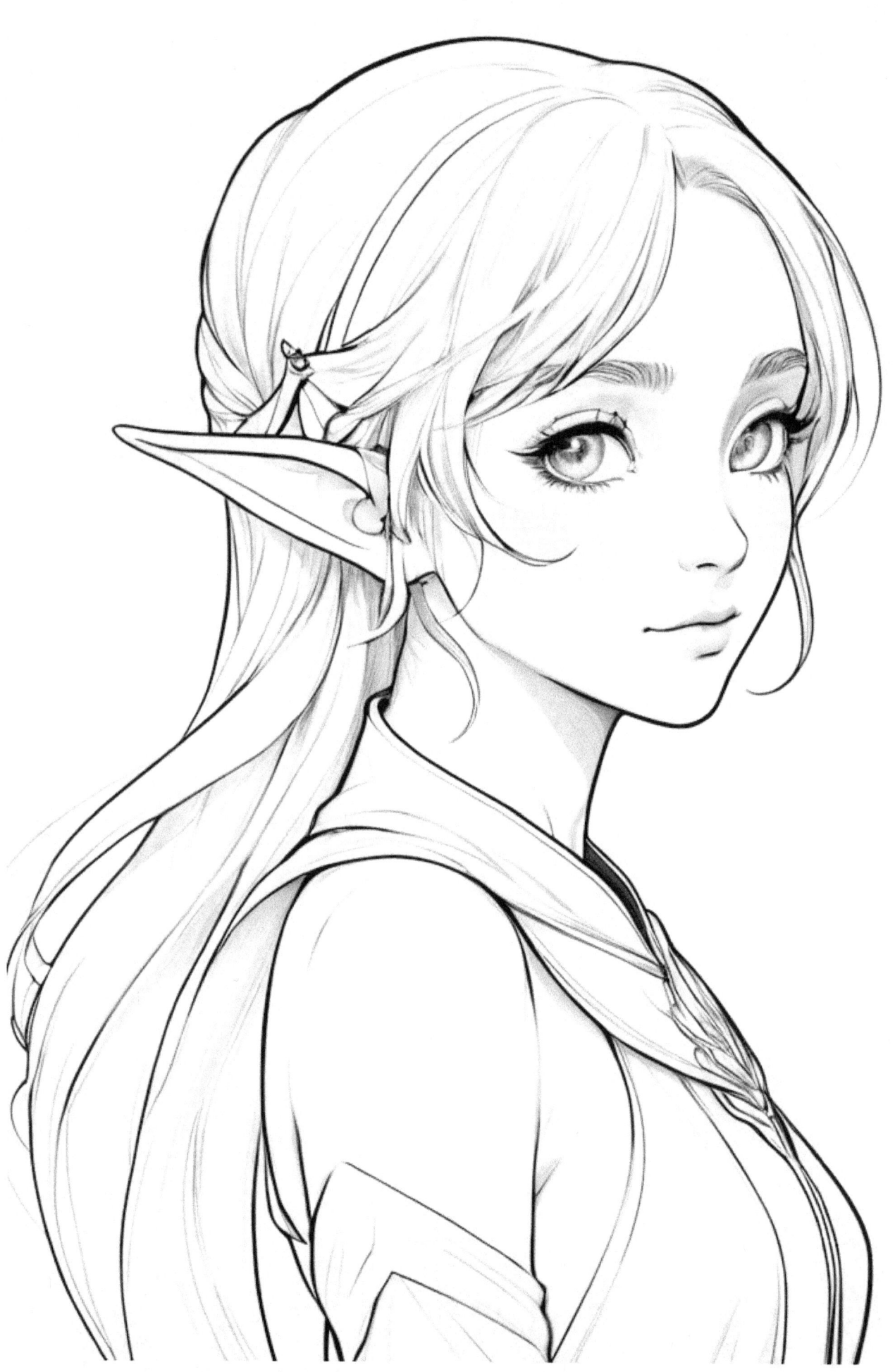

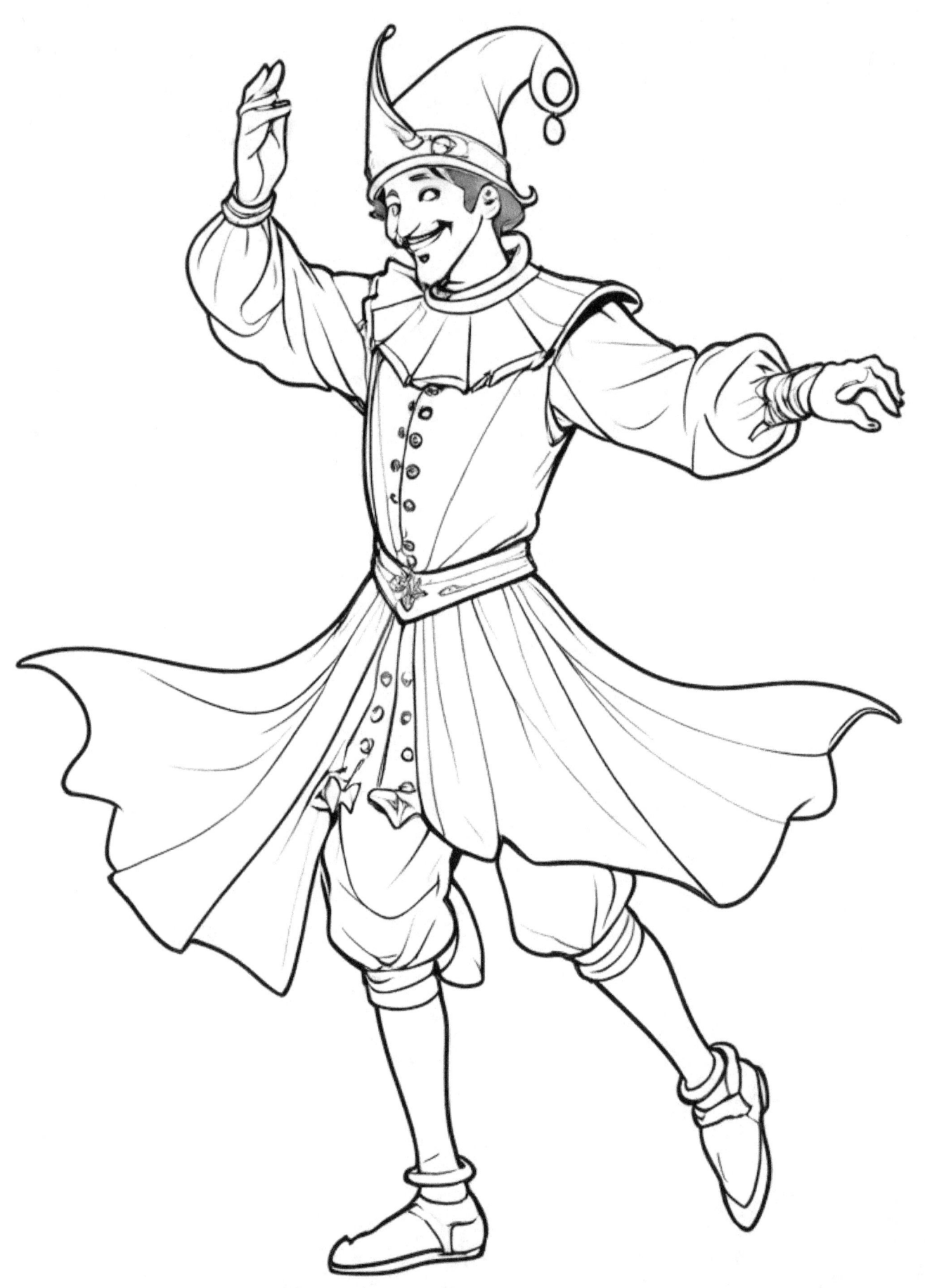

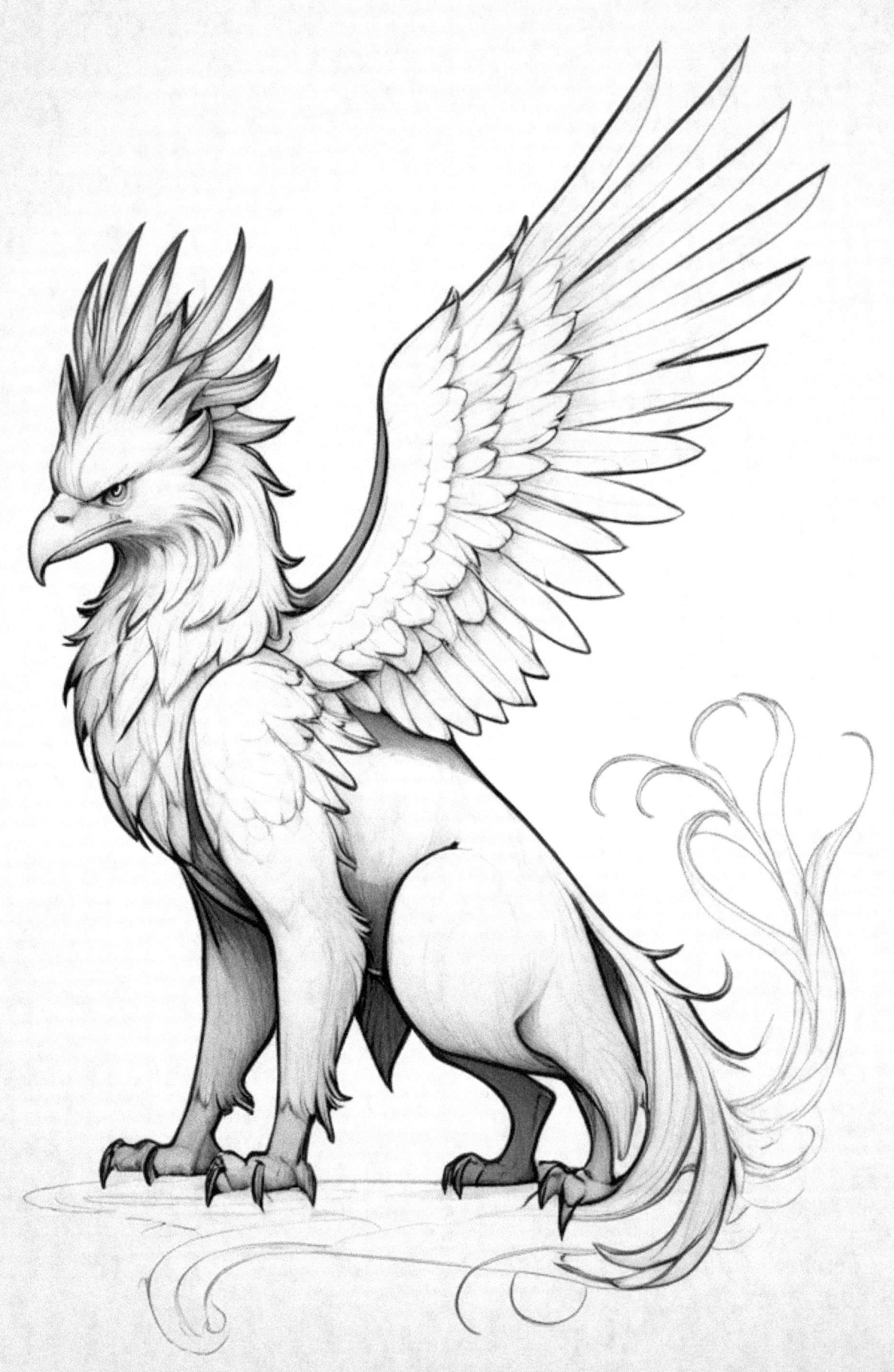

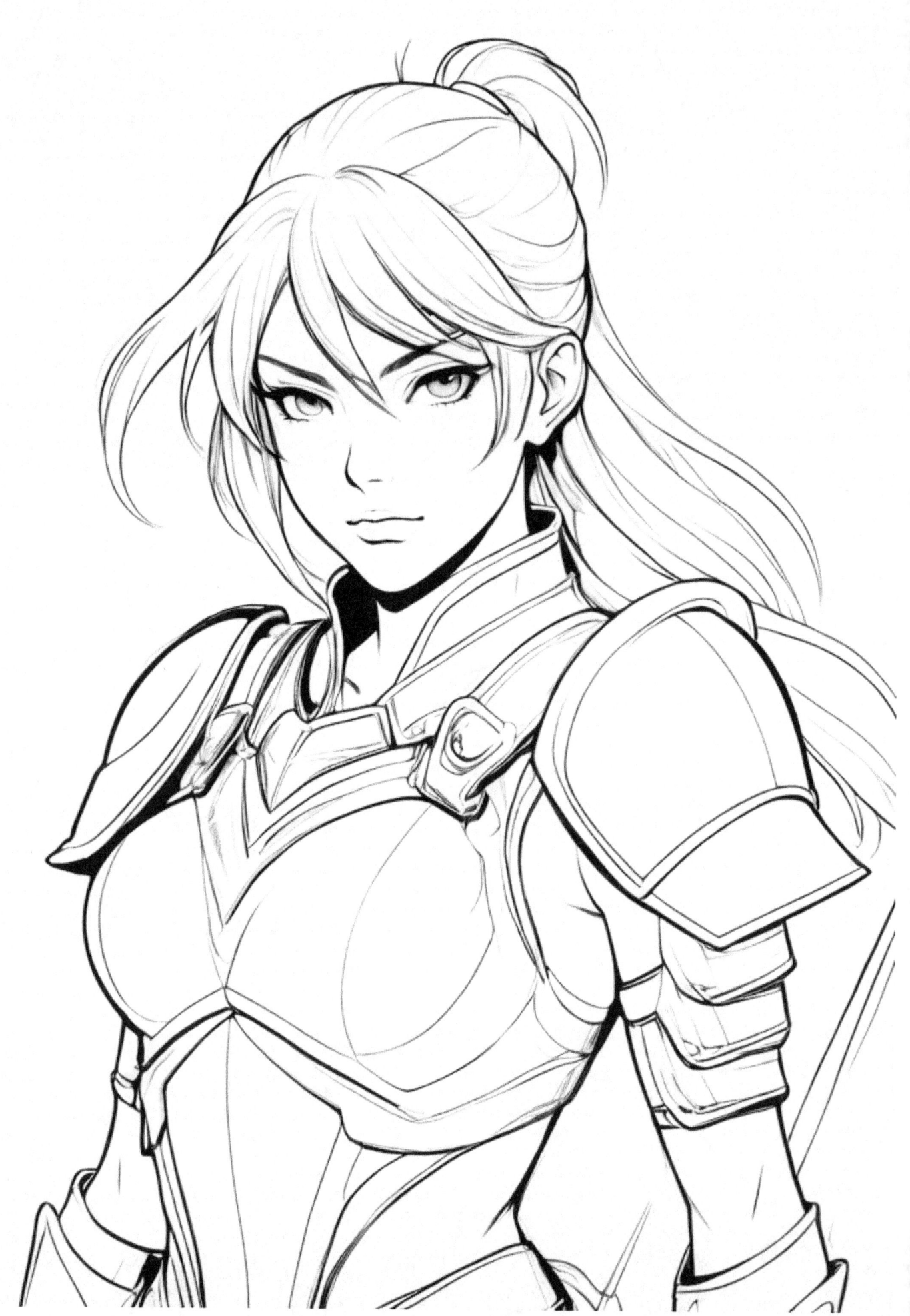

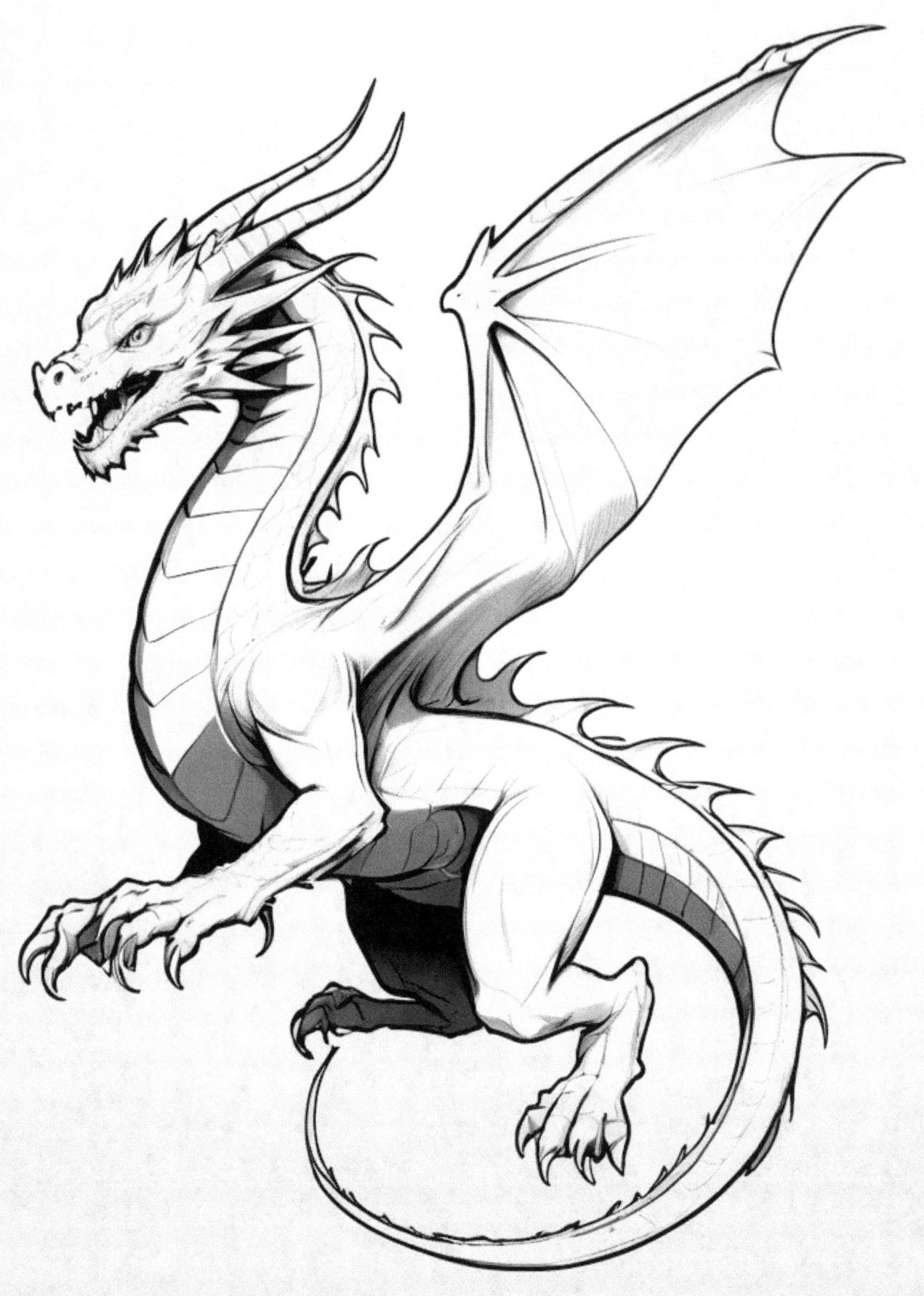

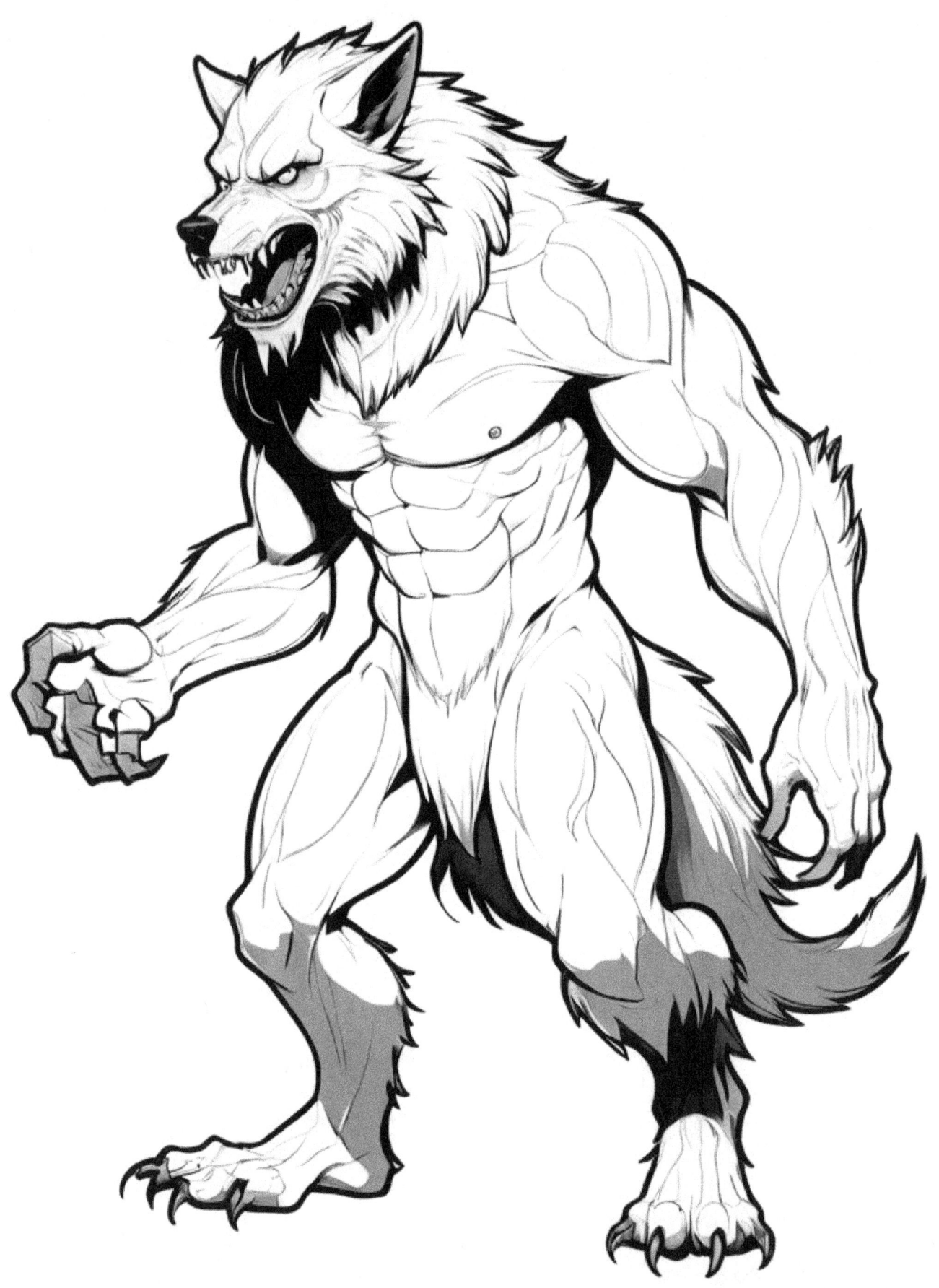

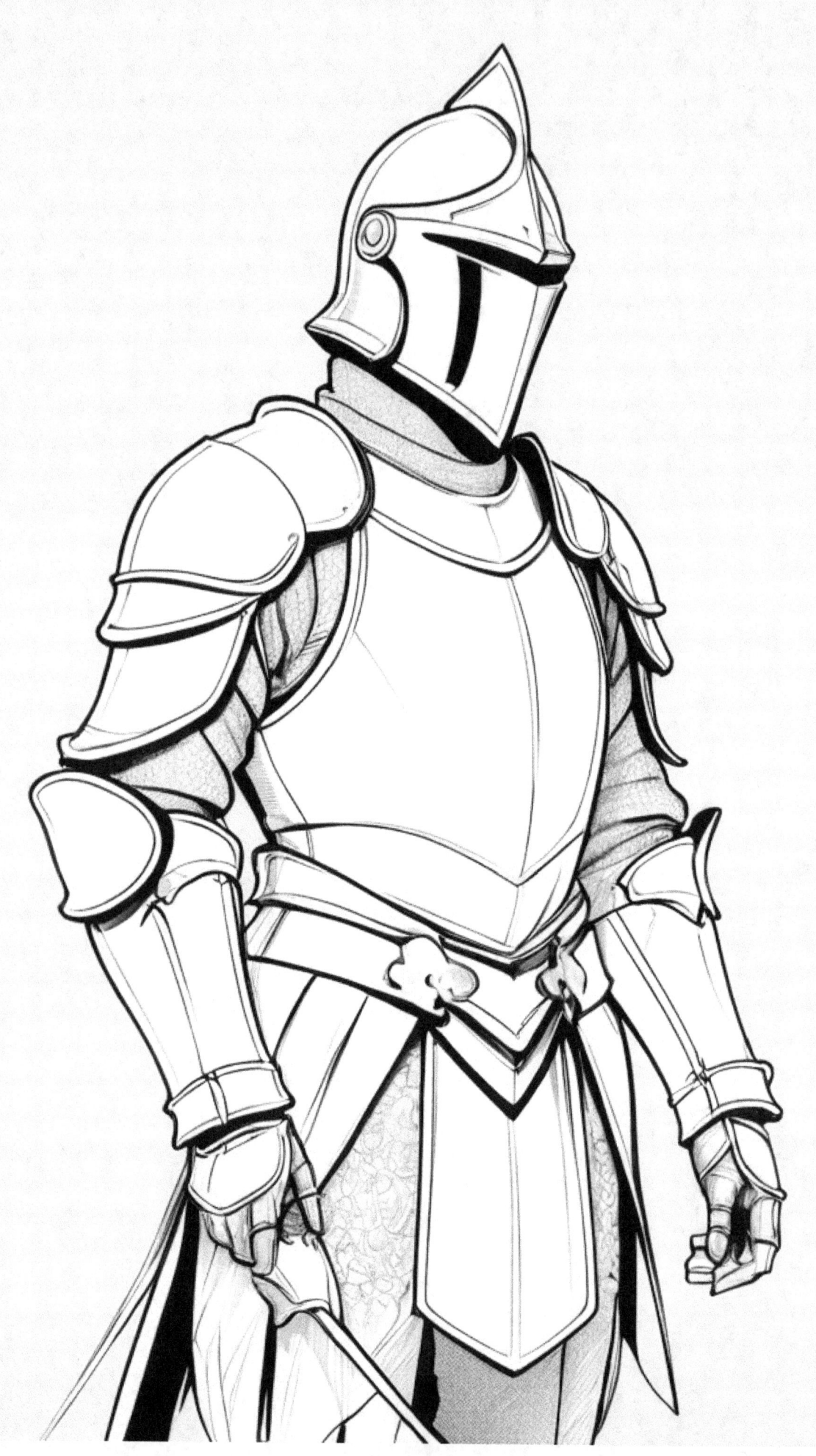

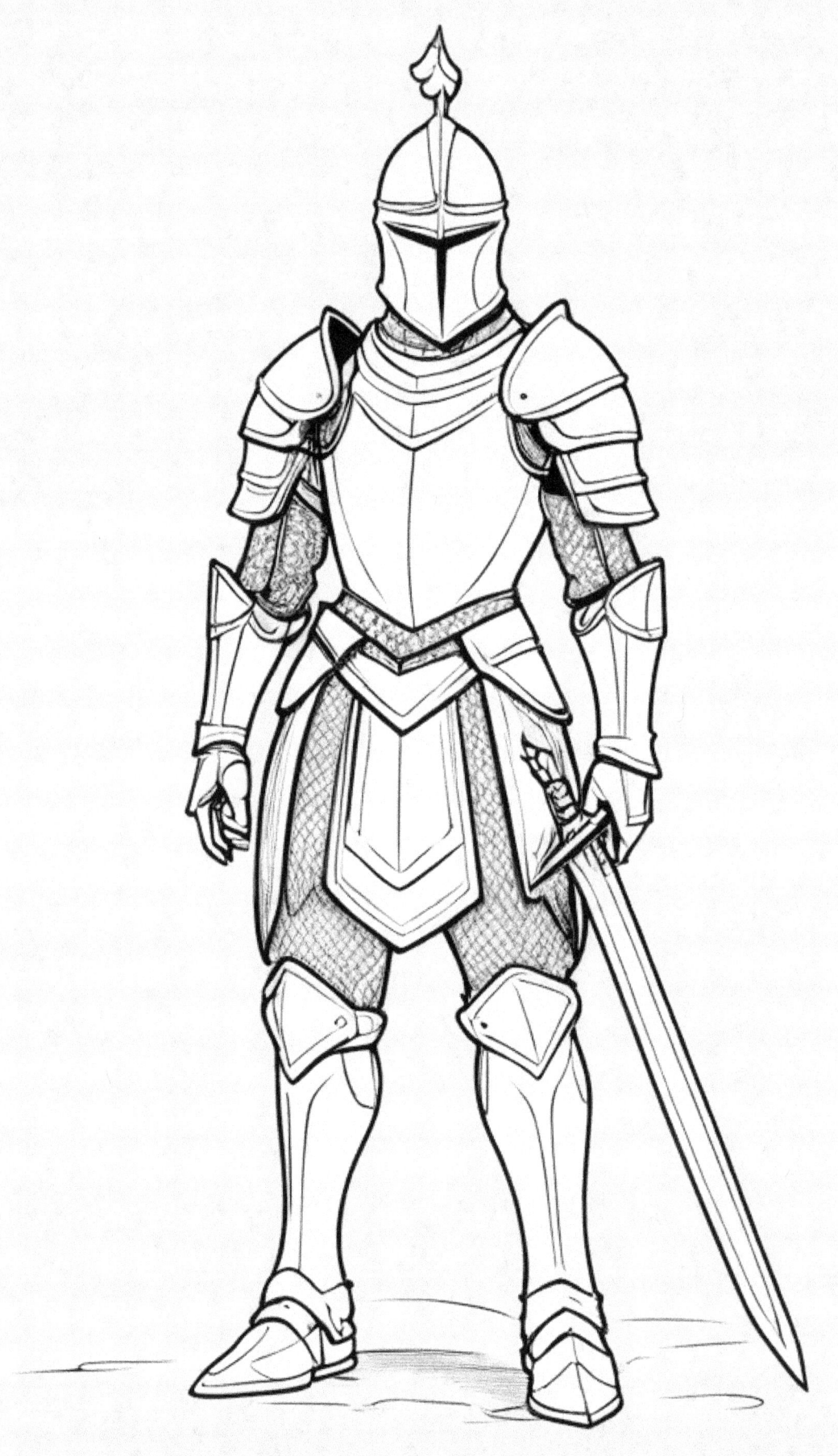

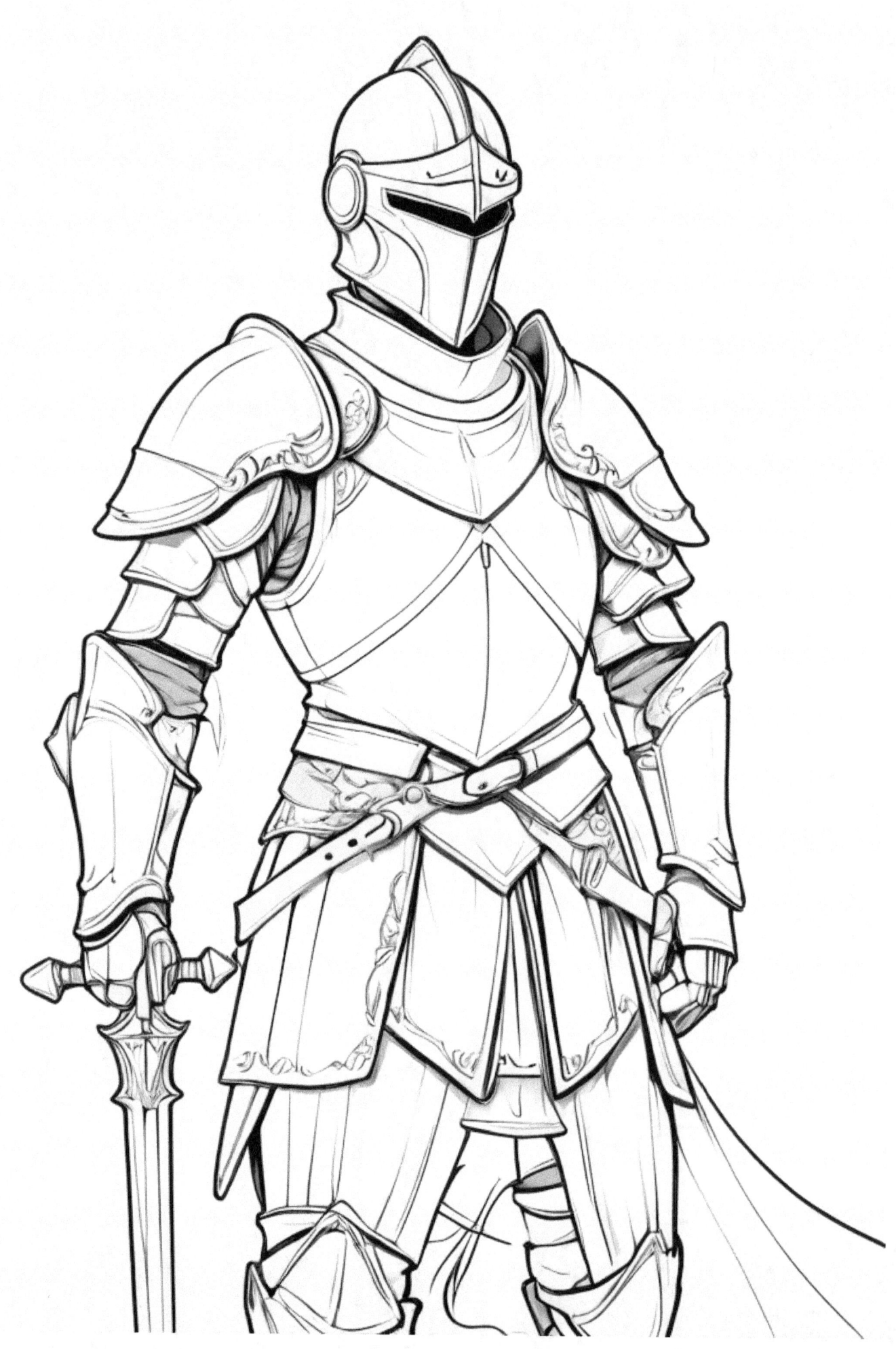

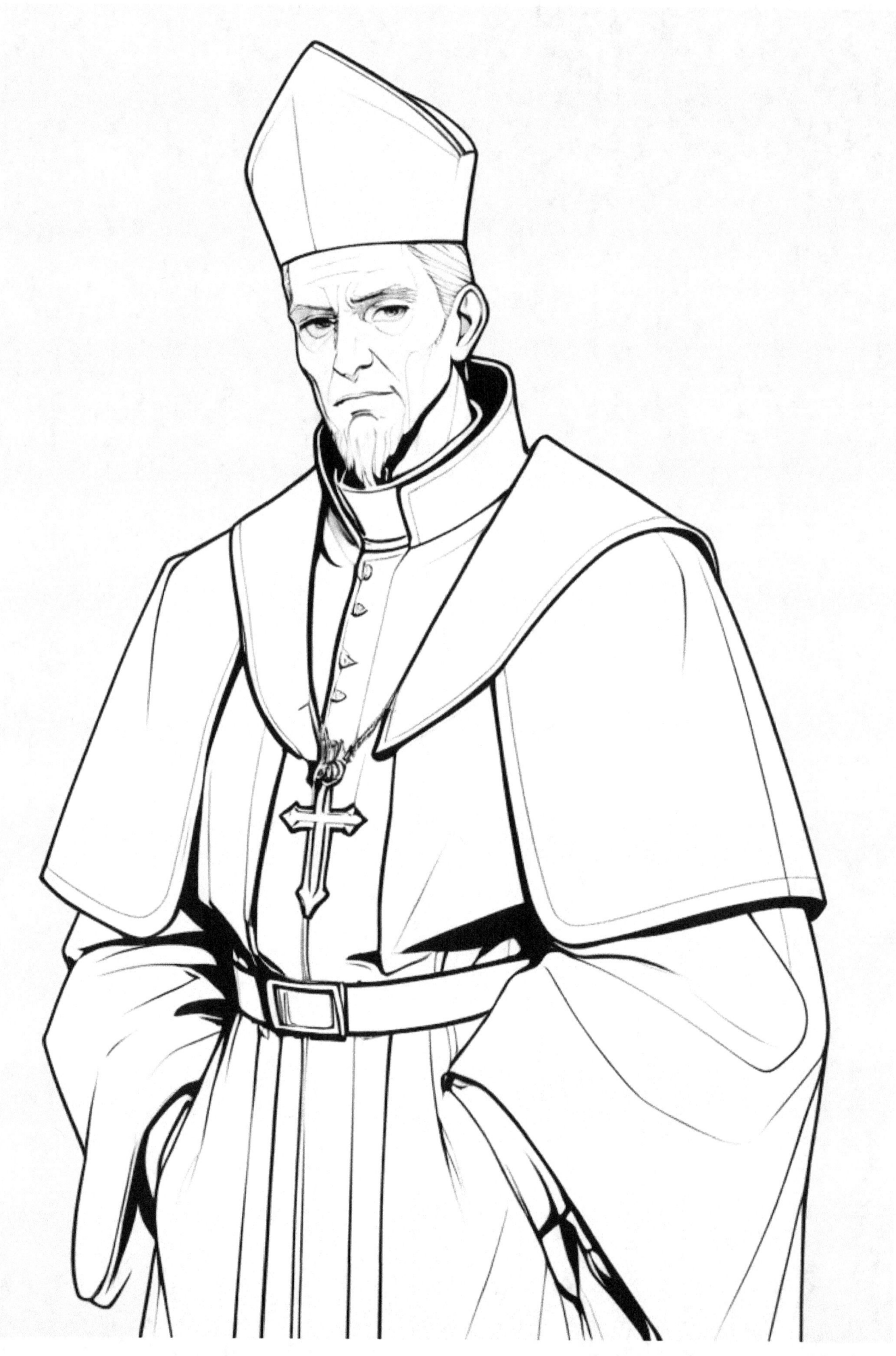

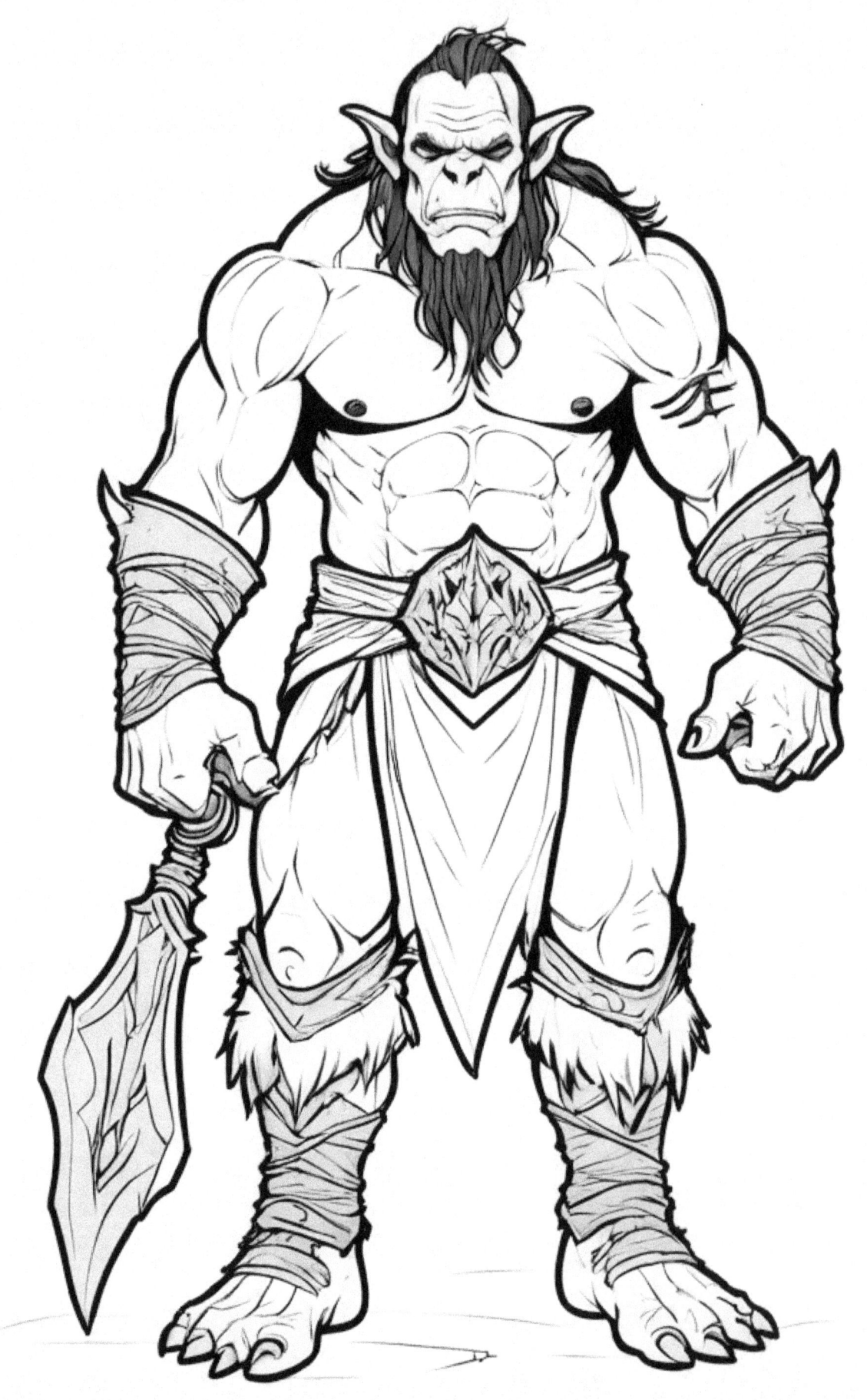

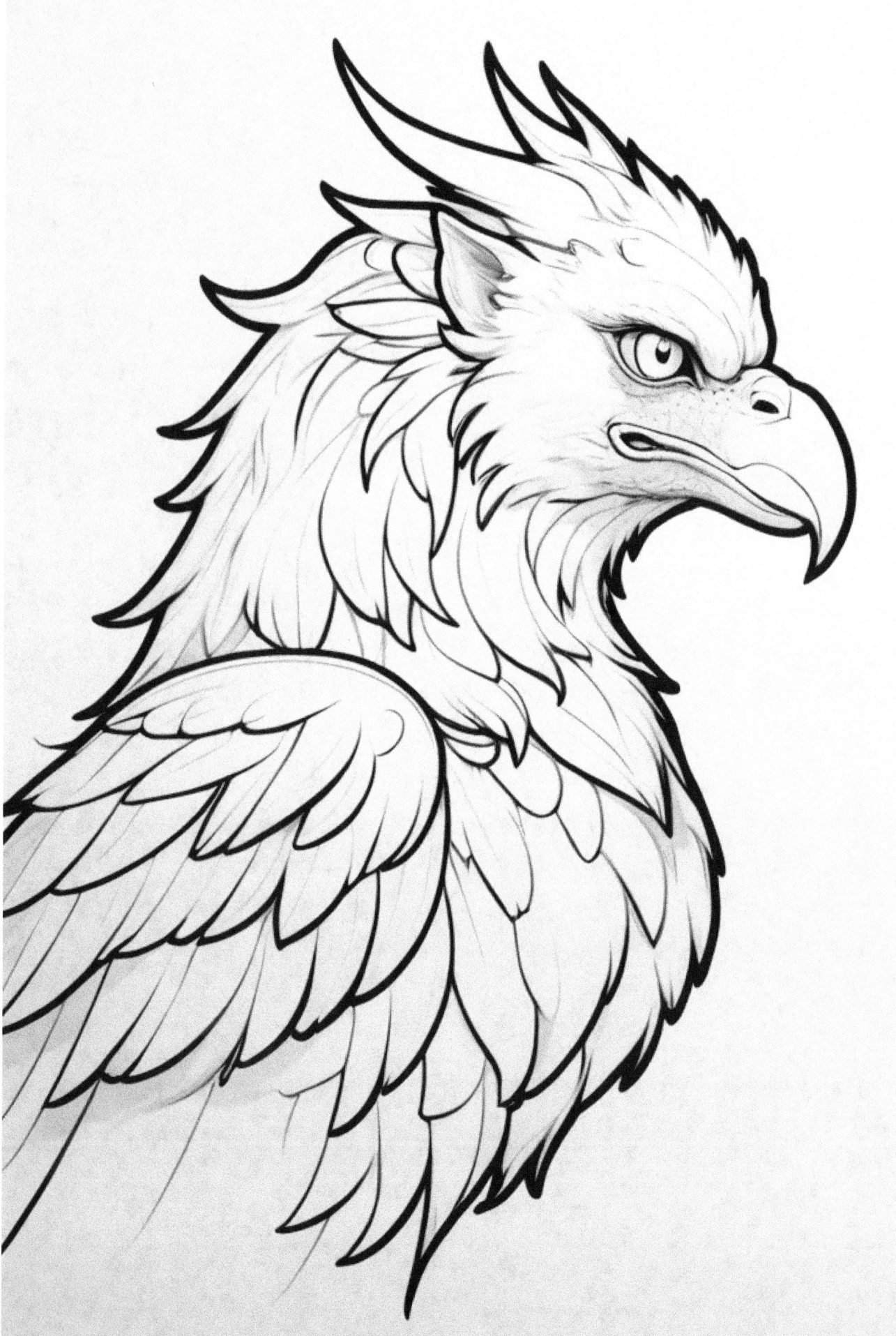

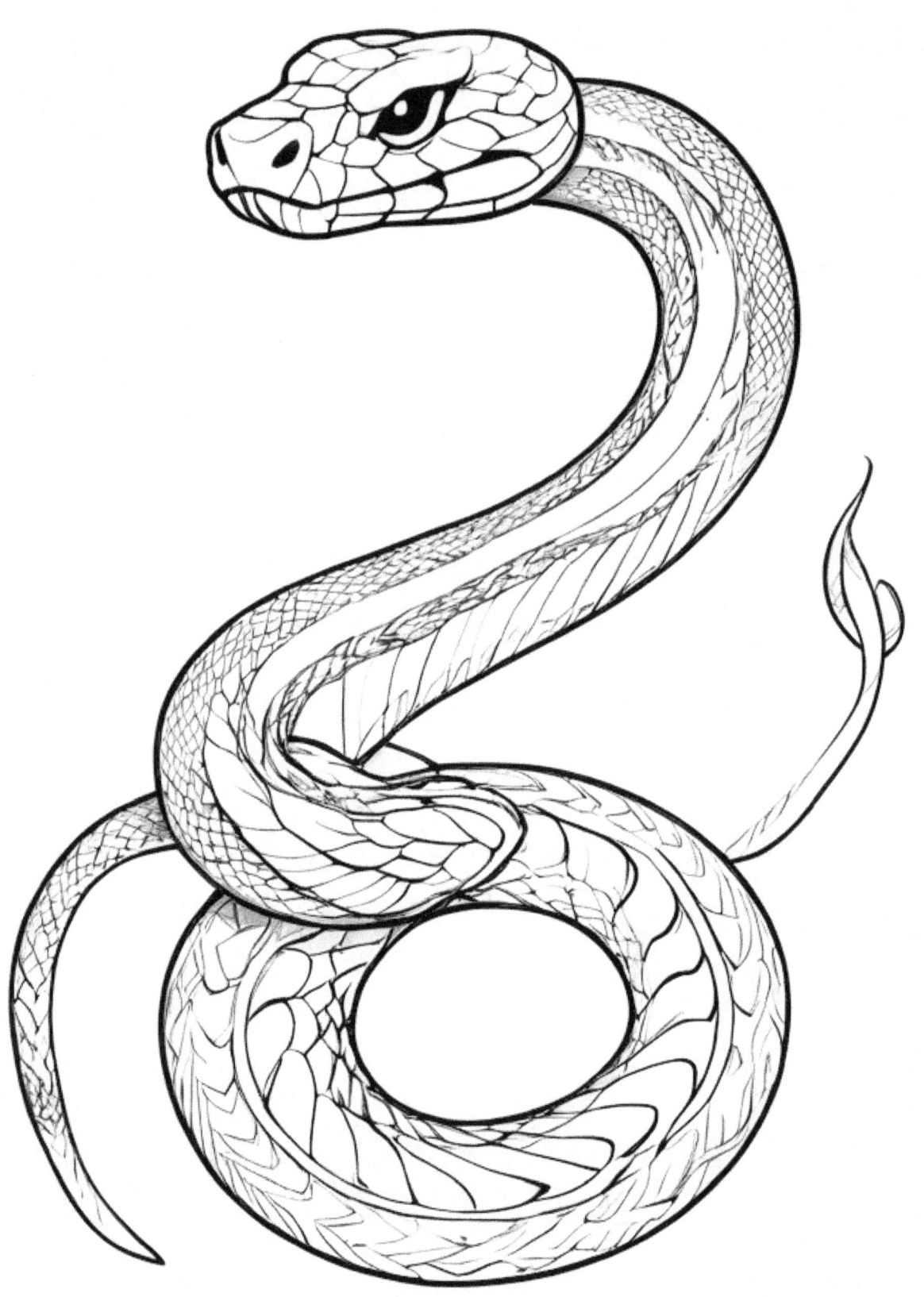

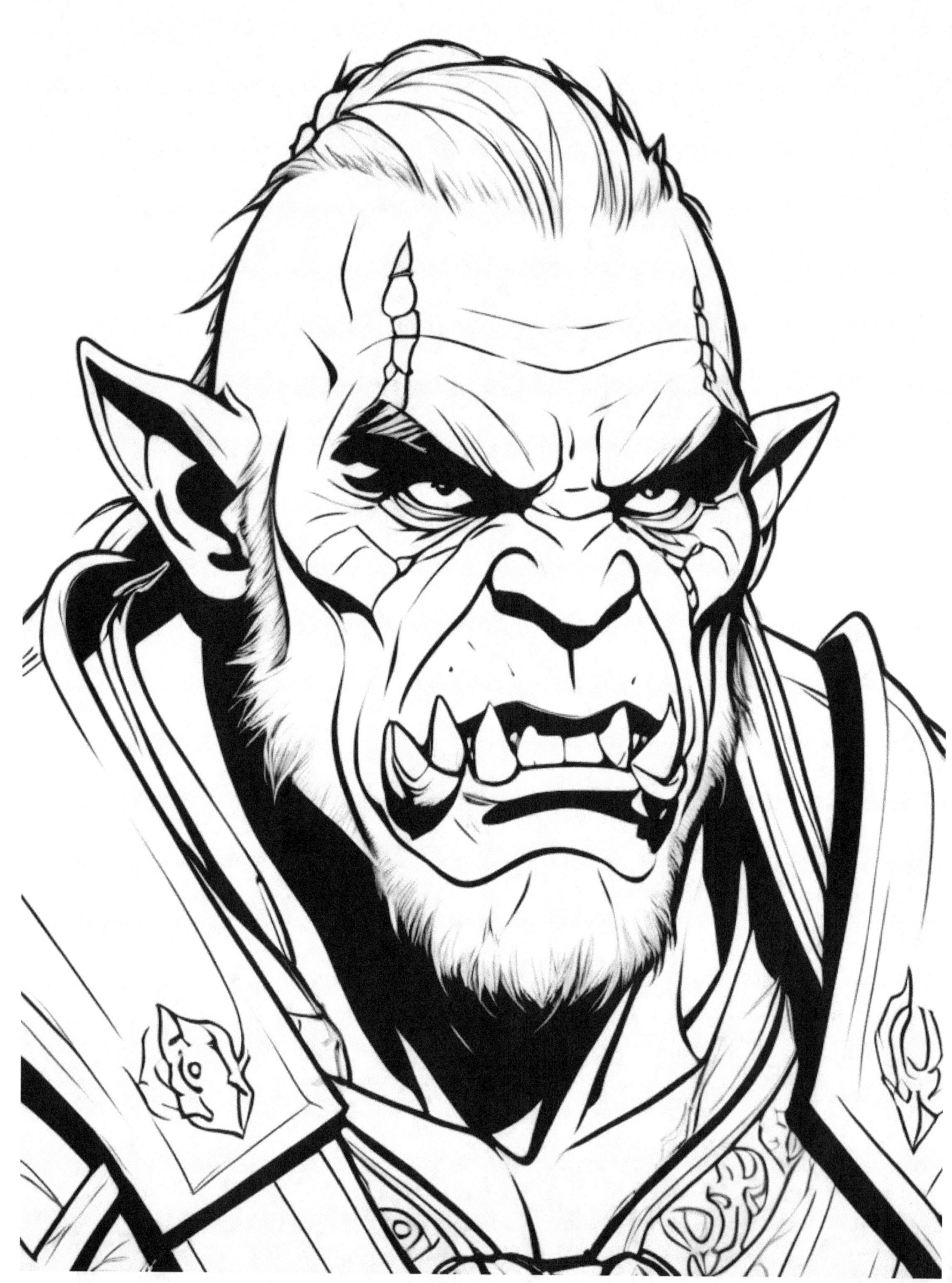

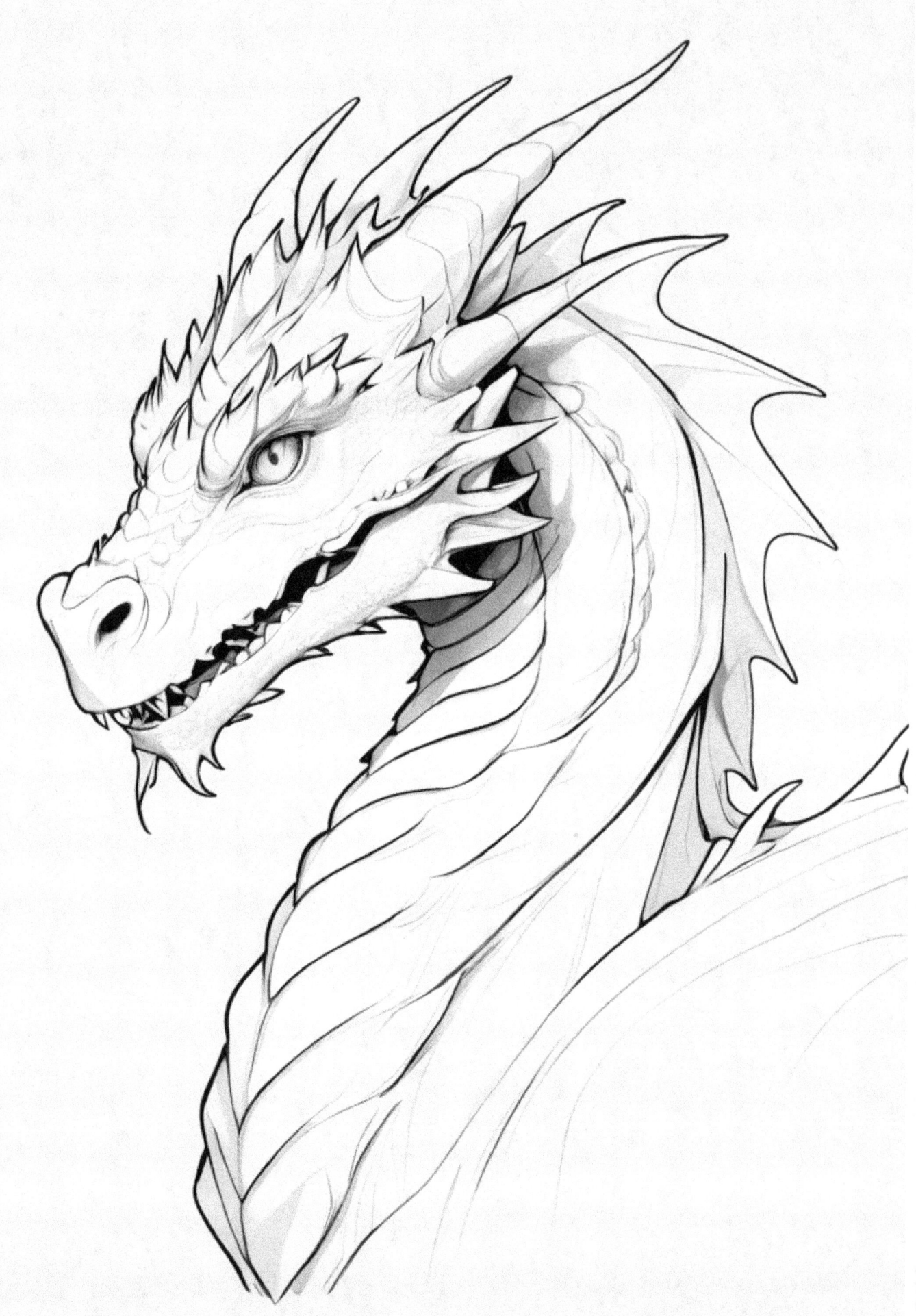

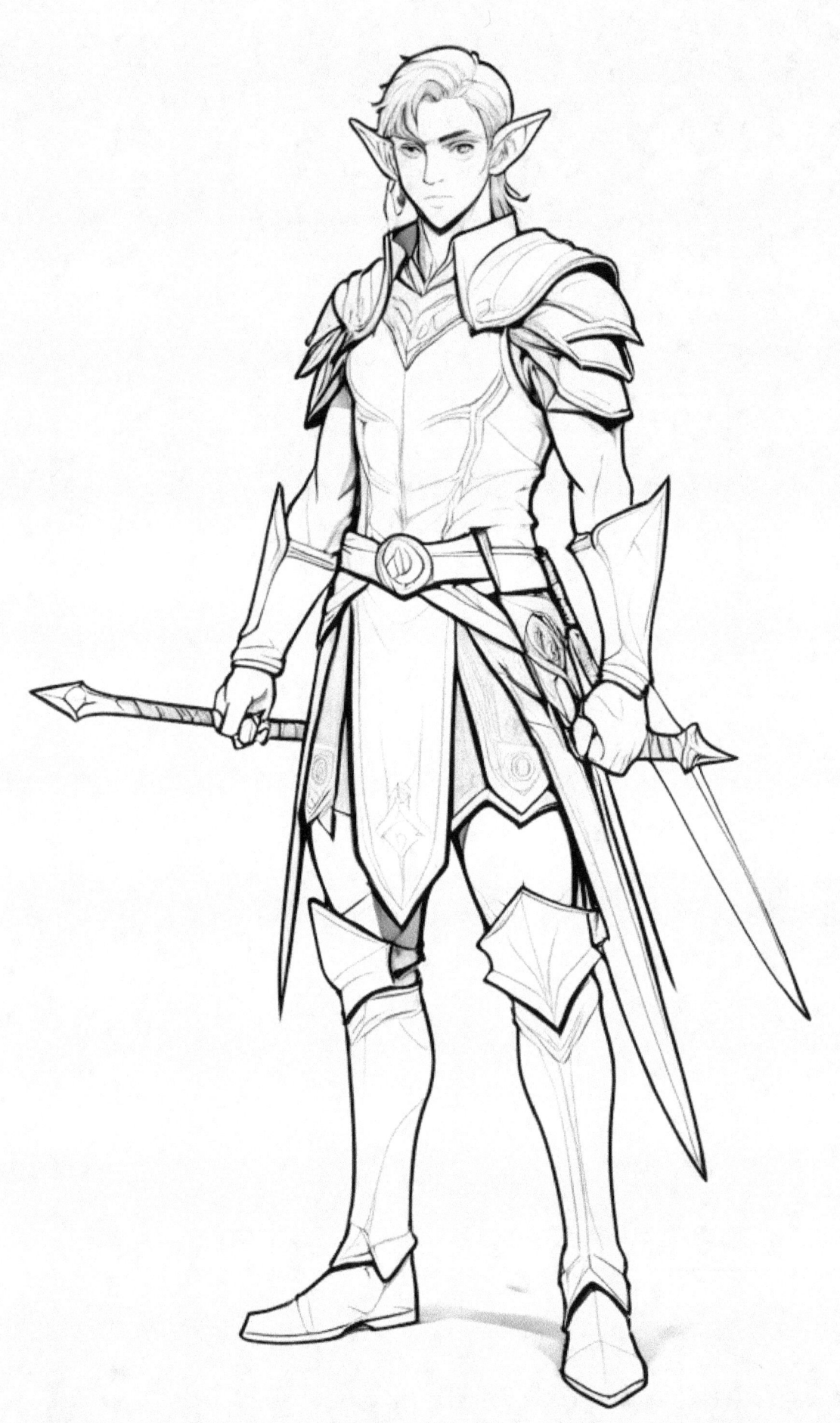

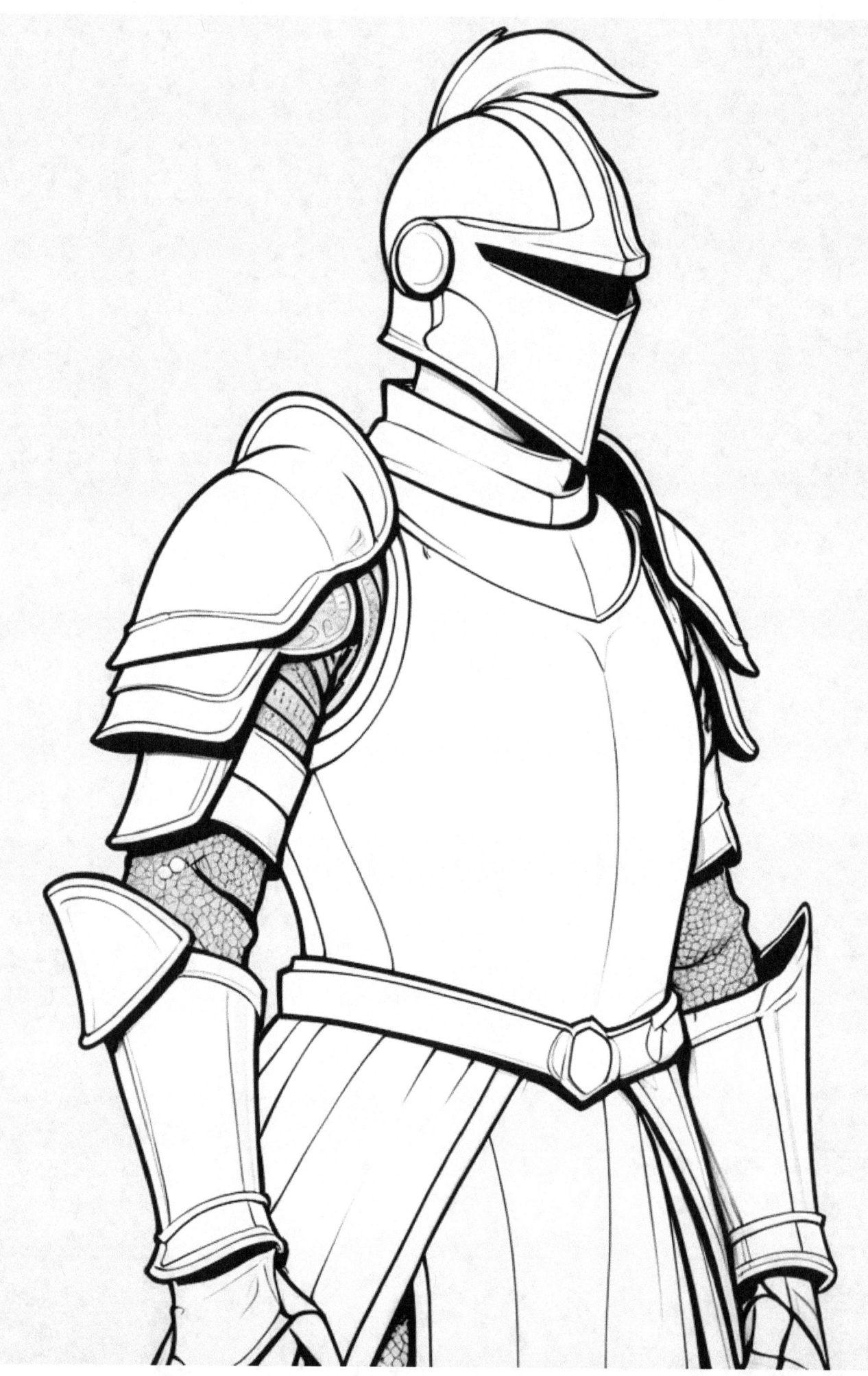

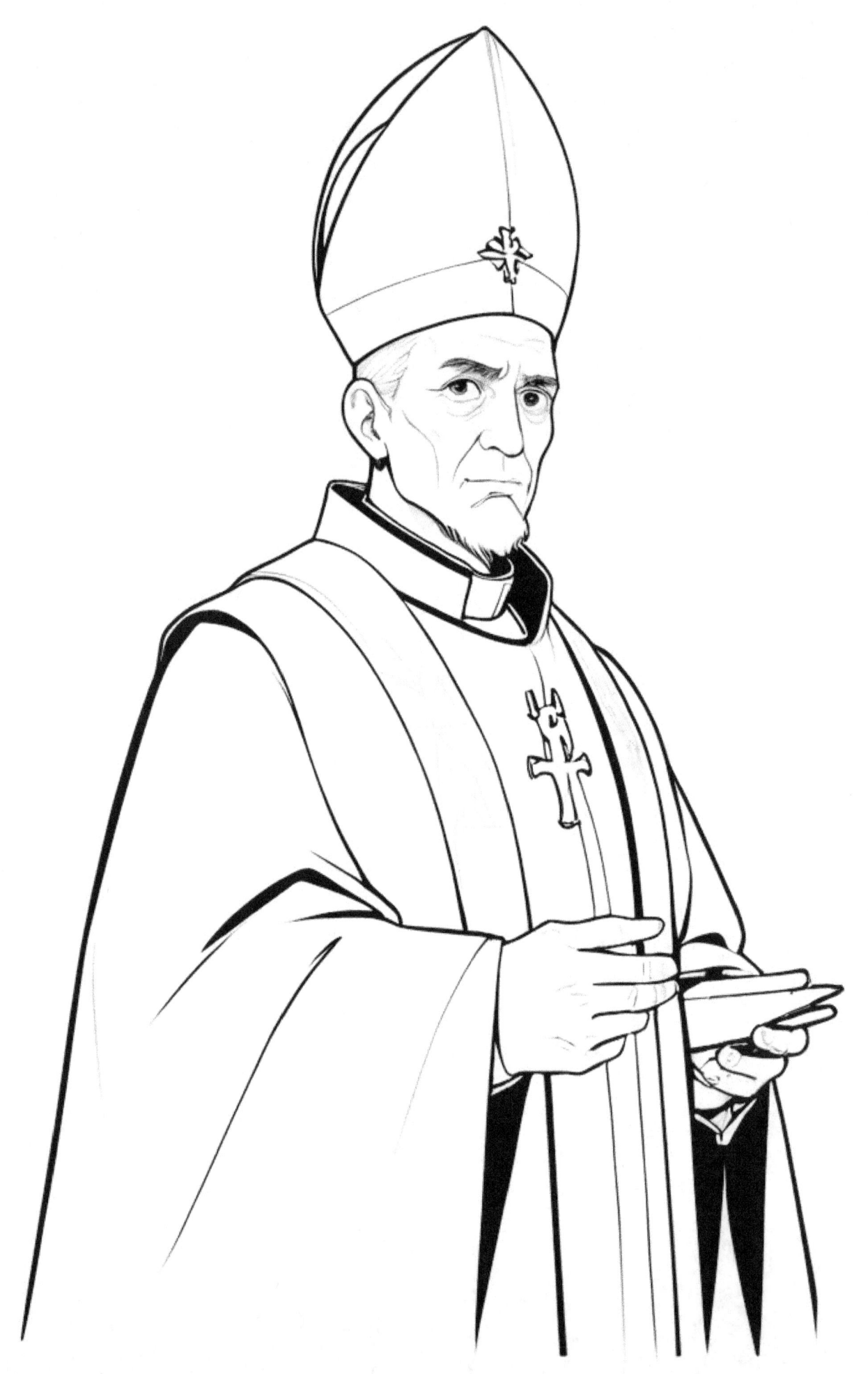

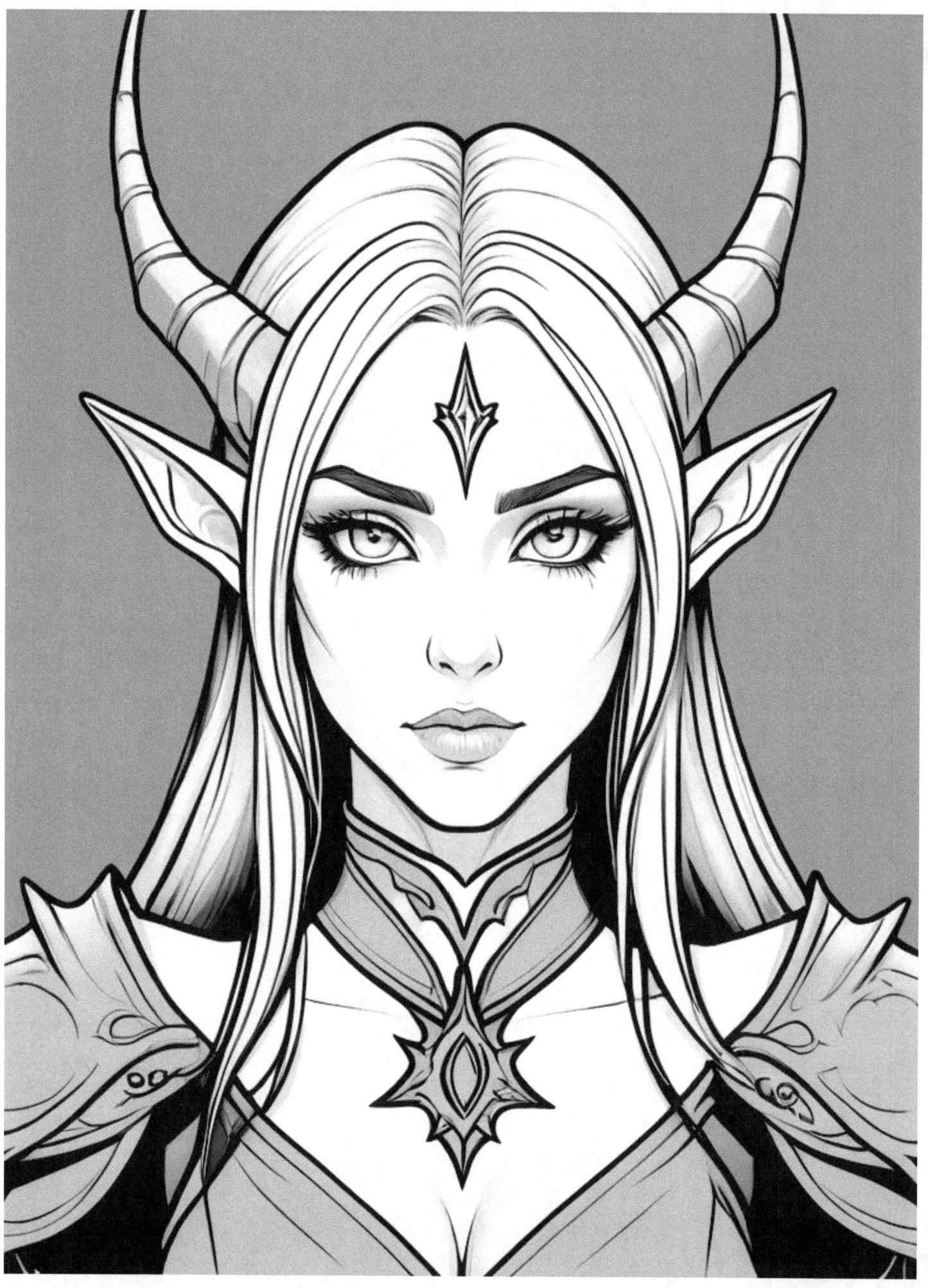